IMPROVING ORGANIZATIONAL HEALTH: AN ANNOTATED BIBLIOGRAPHY OF THE ORGANIZATIONAL DEVELOPMENT LITERATURE

Authors:

Jack McCann, PhD
Mr. Gábor Herédi-Szabó

Lincoln Memorial University School of Business
Harrogate, Tennessee

April, 2012

Author BIOs

Jack T. McCann, Ph. D. (Capella University) is Dean of the School of Business at Lincoln Memorial University in Harrogate, TN. He is also an adjunct professor of business at Kaplan University. His academic research interests are leadership, strategy, sustainability, and ethics. Dr. McCann and his wife Kathy, a nurse, reside in southeastern KY. Contact: jack.mccann@lmunet.edu

Mr. Gábor Herédi-Szabó graduated from Lincoln Memorial University (LMU) in 2010 with a B.B.A. degree majoring in management. He is currently pursuing an MBA degree with concentrations in management and marketing. He also works as a Graduate Assistant at the School of Business at LMU under the direction of Dean Dr. Jack McCann. During his undergraduate studies at LMU, he was a member of the LMU Railsplitter Men's tennis team for four years that won the South Atlantic Conference title in 2010. After finishing his carrier as a student athlete, he is continuing his work with the LMU Railsplitter Tennis Team as a volunteer assistant coach.

Ackerman, L. (2010). The identity effect. *OD Practitioner, 42*(3), pp. 36-42.

The article focuses on organizational identity. It expounds how such identity contributes to organizational effectiveness and business performance. It examines the benefits flexible or fixed and multiple identities. It clarifies the meaning of organizational identity in which uniqueness of every organization, ideology, and value-creating potential are implied.

Subject Terms:

> Organizational ideology
> Organizational effectiveness
> Corporate culture
> Identity-based organizations
> Institutional environment

Adams, J. (2006). Building O.D.C. as an academic discipline: A program director's perspective. *Organization Development Journal, 24*(3), pp. 100-104.

The article focuses on the adaptation of a group scenario related to building organizational development and change as an academic discipline. The process was done in the San Francisco, California area where the participants were placed 15 years in the future in an ideal outcome. Each participant shared his or her perspectives on organizational development.

Subject Terms:

Organizational change
Organizational behavior
Organizational sociology
Organizational structure
Organizational commitment

Adams, J. (2011). Working today as if tomorrow mattered: A challenge to the profession. *OD Practitioner, 43*(4), pp. 33-39.

The article discusses the challenges presented by Mother Nature, economics, and population on the issue of sustainability in the organizational development (OD) profession. It cites the dilemmas and consequences of human activity, depletion of resources, debt problem, and rapid population growth that are all interacting in a complex system. It highlights the approach to successfully make enduring changes and the contribution of OD in promoting the greening of organizations.

Subject Terms:

> Sustainable development
> Organizational change
> Economics
> Population
> Environmental degradation

Adams, J., Royal, C., & Church, A. (2011). From the guest editors: OD and sustainability. *OD Practitioner*, *43*(4), pp. 1-2.

An introduction to the journal is presented in which the editors discuss various reports within the issue on topics including organizational culture for systemic sustainability, sustainability-focused community transition, and the significant role of role of Interorganizational Networks.

Subject Terms:

Corporate culture
Organizational change

Adler, N. J., Brody, L. W., & Osland, J. S. (2000). The Women's Global Leadership Forum: Enhancing one's company's global leadership capabilities. *Human Resource Management*, *39*(2/3), pp. 209.

There is debating question whether women can become leaders in the increasingly global world of the twenty-first century. According to many Chief Executive Officers (CEOs), promoting the best people, whether male or female-into senior leadership positions is a strategic necessity if their companies are to succeed, let alone prosper. This article describes the commitment that one major multinational's CEO made to moving women from around the world into the most senior leadership positions. It describes an organizational development process, led by the CEO that included a targeted survey of both male and female executives, convening a 4 1/2-day Global Leadership Forum, and actively changing the organization based on recommendations generated at the Forum. n convening the Women's Global Leadership Forum, CEO, Dick Shoemate, invited the most senior and highest-potential women in his organization to rise. The process of the Forum and the outcomes that are currently unfolding are proving that neither the company nor the women themselves knew how high they could, should, or would collectively rise.

Subject Terms:

Leadership
Women executives
Organizational change
International business enterprises
Chief executive officers

Agócs, C. (1997). Institutionalized resistance to organizational change: Denial, inaction and repression. *Journal of Business Ethics*, *16*(9), pp. 917-931.

An extensive theoretical and research literature on organizational change and its implementation has been accumulating over the past fifty years. It is customary in this literature to find resistance to change mentioned as an inevitable consequence of organizational change initiatives. Yet there has been little discussion of the nature and forms of resistance that is institutionalized in organizational structure and processes. Furthermore, organization development perspectives on organizational change address management-initiated change, but not change proposed by advocates for the powerless and disadvantaged. Focusing on institutionalized resistance from the standpoint of the advocate of fundamental change, this discussion proposes a typology consisting of a sequence of forms of active resistance to change, from denial through inaction to repression. The typology is illustrated by referring to responses of organizational decision makers to the efforts of employment equity change agents to address issues of systemic discrimination in the work place. The purpose of the typology is to assist change advocates, such as equality seekers, to name, analyze and think strategically about the institutionalized resistance they encounter, and about effective responses to the resistance.

Subject Terms:

> Organizational change
> Sex discrimination in employment
> Industrial management
> Workforce planning
> Industrial sociology
> Organizational research
> Organizational structure
> Organizational behavior
> Work environment
> Organizational sociology
> Resistance to change
> Psychological aspects
> Change agents

Ahearne, M., Lam, S. K., Mathieu, J. E., & Bolander, W. (2010, May). Why are some sales people better at adapting to organizational change? *Journal of Marketing, 74*(3), pp. 65-79.

This study empirically examines the longitudinal influences of salesperson goal orientations on performance trajectories during a planned change intervention that requires learning to answer two questions. First, what is the functional form of salespeople's performance trajectories during a period of change implementation? Second, why are some salespeople better at adapting to change than others? Polynomial growth models show that the average salesperson performance trajectory displays an initial decline, gradual recovery, and eventual re-stabilization. Salesperson learning orientation is related positively to larger initial declines, steeper recovery slopes, and higher re-stabilization levels. In contrast, performance orientation is related positively to smaller initial declines, but shallower recovery slopes and lower re-stabilization levels. The results suggest that successful implementation of planned change interventions largely depends on identifying and appreciating the heterogeneity of individual traits that share meaning with the change. The study has implications on what sales managers should expect in terms of performance losses and gains during change and how managers can predict which salespeople will reap the largest performance benefits from a change intervention.

Subject Terms:

   Sales personnel
   Organizational change
   Marketing research
   Sales management
   Economic development -- Mathematical models
   Employees -- Rating of
   Change
   Sales executives
   Performance
   Adaptation level (Psychology)
   Learning
   Motivation (Psychology)

Author-Supplied Keywords:

   Adaptation to change
   Goal orientation
   Growth modeling
   Organizational change
   Salesperson

Ahmad, K., Veerapandian, K., & Wee Yu, G. (2011). Person-environment fit: The missing link in the organizational culture-commitment relationship. *International Journal of Business & Management*, *6*(11), pp. 11-20.

The purpose of this study was to investigate the mediating effect of person-environment fit on the relationship between organizational culture and organizational commitment. Data were obtained from full-time employees who were working in private and public sectors from various organizations in Malaysia (n = 204). Person-environment fit was found to be a significant mediator of the relationship between organizational culture and organizational commitment. This has wide-ranging implications for organizational development consultants who intend to shape the culture of various organizations, on the assumption that certain organizational cultures directly lead to certain desirable employee outcomes. Managers need to pay attention to not only their organizational culture such as training, rewards, teamwork and communication, but to also ensure that they are aimed towards improving the fit between individuals and their work environment. Whereas previous research tends to look at P-E fit as a predictor of employee outcomes, this is one of the first few studies to provide evidence of P-E fit as a mediator of the relationship between organizational culture and organizational commitment.

Subject Terms:

    Corporate culture
    Organizational commitment
    Work attitudes
    Work environment
    Organizational change
    Industrial management
    Attention

Ainsworth, D. (2010). Is there OD for me? *OD Practitioner*, *42*(3), pp. 43-47.

The article speculates on the intricacies of organization development (OD). It expounds on how organization development is implied to large and wealthy organizations. The author then presents his experience as co-owner of a small business wherein elements of organization design and function for organizational effectiveness are regarded. The author then emphasizes that OD does not only applies at the forefront of big business, but also for small ones.

Subject Terms:

Organizational change
Organizational effectiveness
Strategic planning
Business development
Business planning

Akdere, M., & Altman, B. A. (2009). An organization development framework in decision making: Implications for practice. *Organization Development Journal, 27*(4), pp. 47-56.

The action research model, as an Organization Development (OD) intervention method, has the potential to enhance the organizational decision making process. In this paper, we illustrate how Cummings and Worley's (2009) conceptualization of the action research model of planned change can be applied to decision making in two distinct ways depending on the diagnosed problem: in making a specific decision or in determining which decision-making strategy or strategies should be used for a range of decisions.

Subject Terms:

    Decision-making
    Discrete choice models
    Decision support systems
    Strategic planning
    Action research
    Decision making in international relations
    Evaluation research (Social action programs)
    Social science research
    Social action

Akdere, M., & Azevedo, R. E. (2006). Agency theory implications for efficient contracts in organization development. *Organization Development Journal, 24*(2), pp. 43-54.

This paper presents an analysis of the Organization Development (O.D.) function in organizations in light of the precepts and utility of agency theory. The paper further examines how the roles of 'principals' and 'agents' complicate the change and improvement processes and experience, and challenge the role of O.D. professionals. This paper contributes to our understanding of why, even with what appear to be the best of intentions on all sides, the principals and agents in organizations may interact to cause failure and outlines the implications of this dynamic process within the organization.

Subject Terms:

      Organizational research
      Organizational change
      Agency theory
      Communication in organizations
      Performance standards
      Industrial psychology

Akhtar, M. F., & Cozic, C. (2010). Unleashing innovation through HR/OD Collaboration. *OD Practitioner, 42*(4), pp. 47-51.

The article discusses the significance of human resource (HR) and organization development (OD) collaboration that can be a springboard for innovation to boost business performance. It cites HR and OD roles, as well as corresponding competencies, which highlights their differences. It details the design process and planning sessions of OD and HR for an ongoing business transformation.

Subject Terms:

Management
Organizational change
Personnel management
Technological innovations
Organizational effectiveness
Strategic planning

Aldulaimi, S., & Sailan, M. (2012). The national values impact on organizational change in public organizations in Qatar. *International Journal of Business & Management, 7*(1), pp. 182-191.

This paper aims to investigate the impact of Hofstede's five dimensions of national values (Power Distance, Individualism, Uncertainty Avoidance, Masculinity, and Long-Term Orientation) on commitment to organizational change and individual readiness for change. No empirical research of the influence of national values on organizational change was conducted. Structural equation model employed in particular confirmatory factor analysis and path analysis procedures was used to test the hypothesized model. Findings of this study offer valuable insights on why cultural values should be differentiated as they relate to different individual readiness and commitment to change. The findings of this study will be useful to the policy makers and organizations that plan to accomplish change initiatives, particularly those in Arabic region. Managers at international corporations can also benefit from this study if they have business dealings with the people from this region. The study is among the first that investigates the issue of change implementation from the perspective of national cultural values.

Subject Terms:

> Organizational change
> International business enterprises
> Organizational structure
> Structural equation modeling
> Cultural values

Alshbiel, S., & Al-Awawdeh, W. M. (2011). Internal social responsibility and its impact on job commitment: Empirical study on Jordanian Cement Manufacturing Co. *International Journal of Business & Management*, *6*(12), pp. 94-102.

The purpose of this paper is to explore the relationship between internal social responsibility and job commitment from a sample of 131-employees in Jordanian Cement Manufacturing Co. This study adopts the descriptive analytical methodology both theoretical and practical. Results showed a positive statistically strong relationship between the organizational structure and job commitment. Further, results also showed a negative relationship between the managerial policies and organizational commitment; and no statistically significant relationship between corporate innovation and job commitment. This study concludes with a number of recommendations that call for clearly identified management policies; enhancement of the innovation process at a larger scale that motivates job commitment among employees. This study calls for further studies that measure the effect of innovation, as one of internal social responsibility dimensions, on job commitment in industrial companies such as the Arab Potash Co. and Jordan Petroleum Refinery Co. to find out whether they agree or disagree with results from this study.

Subject Terms:

Organizational commitment
Organizational structure
Organizational change
Social responsibility

Alter, S. (2011). Market smarter. *Journal of Property Management, 76*(6), pp. 14.

The article offers the author's insights regarding the marketing strategies to strengthen the company's market position. The author states some ideas to be considered for the game plan such as not to settle organizational changes until the things calm down, go for the magic, and inventory the skills. She mentions some factors to improve one's skills such as budgeting, reconciliation, and monthly reporting.

Subject Terms:

> Marketing strategy
> Organizational change
> Marketing management
> Life skills
> Self-help techniques

Anderson, P. T., & Ovaice, G. (2006). Strategic organization development: A seat at the table. *Organization Development Journal, 24*(4), pp. 29-37.

Somewhere in O.D.'s history, the organization seems to have gotten lost. This article outlines why O.D. practitioners must become business partners and suggest ways they can be invited to the strategic table. The ambiguity associated with business strategy and what it means to be strategic is discussed. The paper ties the proud traditions of O.D. with the current realities and complex environment in which companies must survive today. Lastly, a process to develop a sound O.D. strategy that is linked to strategic outcomes of the business is proposed. Most will agree that O.D. must become more strategic in the way change is facilitated. However, we must also begin a dialogue about how O.D. practitioners can become strategic partners. One cannot happen without the other.

Subject Terms:

    Organizational change
    Organization
    Management
    Strategic planning
    Organizational behavior
    Joint ventures
    Business planning

Andreadis, N. (2009). Learning and organizational effectiveness: A systems perspective. *Performance Improvement*, *48*(1), pp. 5-11.

The challenge for leaders today is to create and develop the capability of their organization. Leaders must perceive and manage their organization as a dynamic, open system where learning is the core competence underlying innovation, growth, and sustainability. Creating a culture of learning is the first work of leadership. This article presents a practical framework in which to consider organizational effectiveness, emphasizing the critical role of systems thinking and learning theory in organizational development.

Subject Terms:

    Organizational
    Technological innovations
    Leadership
    Organizational effectiveness
    Organizational change
    Learning

Arena, M. J. (2009). Understanding large group intervention processes: A complexity theory perspective. *Organization Development Journal, 27*(1), pp. 49-64.

This article evaluates large group interventions as organizational change methods that address more adequately than traditional models the complexity, unpredictability, and turbulence associated with today's organizations. Large group interventions are presented as a means to facilitate organizational change from a complexity science perspective. The author argues that such interventions increase an organization's potential for amplifying ideas and generating radical change through self-organization: By equipping organizations to rely on their ability to reference and rearrange existing resources into more complex states, they create a balance between structure and information flow. The article concludes with a discussion of the implications of large group interventions for organizational change.

Subject Terms:

Organizational change
Job enrichment
Information resources
Personnel management
Large group instruction
Complexity (Philosophy)
Self-organizing systems

Armenakis, A., & Bedeian, A. (1999). Organizational change: A review of theory and research in the 1990's. *Journal of Management, 25*(3), pp. 293-315.

This article examines the theoretical and empirical organizational change literature over the period of 1990-early 1998. Research dealing with monitoring affective and behavioral reactions to change is also reviewed. In closing, general observations and suggestions for future research are offered and it is concluded that the organizational change literature continues to be responsive to the dynamics of contemporary workplace demands. To make the present effort manageable, we made two decisions. The first dealt with the literature base to be surveyed. Given the breadth of the 1987 and 1989 yearly reviews as contrasted with the specialized focus of the 1992 review, we primarily consider theory and research on organizational change, in general, through early 1998, focusing on work since 1990. The first research theme, dealing with content issues, largely focuses on the substance of contemporary organizational changes. Research in this category has typically attempted to define factors that comprise the targets of both successful and unsuccessful change efforts and how these factors relate to organizational effectiveness. The second research theme to be discussed, dealing with contextual issues, principally focuses on forces or conditions existing in an organization's external and internal environments.

Subject Terms:

>   Management
>   Organizational structure
>   Personnel changes
>   Organizational change
>   Work environment
>   Industrial efficiency
>   Organizational effectiveness
>   Organizational sociology

Armstrong, T. R. (2004). New and emerging issues and theories in OD. *Organization Development Journal, 22*(2), pp. 1-2.

Introduces a series of articles focused on philosophical reflections of organization development (OD). Discussion of the direction the OD field is taking; Protection of the normative core of OD while adding to its peripheries; Proposal of a future resting on four value assumptions argued as crucial to the future of OD and of the world.

Subject Terms:

    Organizational change
    Organization
    Organizational behavior
    Organizational sociology
    Organizational structure

Armstrong, T. R. (2006). Building O.D.C as an academic discipline: An O.D.C Practitioner's Perspective. *Organization Development Journal, 24*(3), pp. 110-111.

The article focuses on establishing organizational development and change on the standpoint of organization development practitioner. The author points out on the history in terms of how organizational development practitioners have developed and been educated in the U.S. The author argues that the there are challenges facing organization change as a discipline and suggested actions that need to be addressed by the discipline.

Subject Terms:

     Organizational behavior
     Organizational change
     Organizational learning
     Organizational sociology
     Universities & colleges
     Curricula

Armstrong, T. R. (2009). Learning from failures in O.D. consulting. *Organization Development Journal, 27*(1), pp. 71-77.

Focusing on the positive is not just a recent trend in O.D. it is argued, but has been with us since the beginning. The failure-phobic orientation of O.D. and giving a positive spin to O.D. work may have had its purpose, but we are paying a price for our rose-colored glasses by denying our existential condition and the realities of our practice. There is much to be learned from our failures and we need to share them so others will not make the same mistakes.

Subject Terms:

Organizational change
Business failures
Leadership
Development leadership
Failure (Psychology)
Phobias
Ability testing
Education leadership

Awbrey, S. M. (2005). General education reform as organizational change: The importance of integrating cultural and structural change. *Journal of General Education, 54*(1), pp. 1-21.

The article provides a lens for readers to think about general education reform as organizational change. The author highlights the social and cultural elements that can enhance or impede change efforts and describes different models that can help change agents in their quest for sustained and sustainable reform. The author examines how higher education administrators and faculty can obtain more successful and sustainable reform outcomes by applying knowledge derived from literature and research on organizational change and by recognizing the importance of systematically integrating cultural and structural approaches to change. The paper concludes with the theoretical and practical integration of cultural and structural change processes.

Backner, M. C., Lazaric, N., Nelson, R. R., & Winter, S. G. (2005, Sept. 5).
Applying organizational routine in understanding organizational change.
Industial and Corporate Change, 14(5), pp. 775-791.

Organizational routines are considered basic components of organizational behavior repositories of organizational capabilities (Nelson& Winter, 1982). They do, therefore, hold one of the key to understand organizational change. The article focuses on how the concept of organizational routines can be applied in empirical research to understand organizational change. We identify problems encountered in such research and present proposals for how to deal with them, in order to advance our knowledge of routines and out understanding of organizational change. Developing these themes, we also introduce the articles in the special section 'Toward an Operationalization of the Routines Concept'.

Subject Terms:

Organizational behavior
Organizational change
Organizational structure
Corporation culture
Group decision making
Operation definitions

Baker, T. (2009). The new employee-employer relationship model. *Organization Development Journal, 27*(1), pp. 27-38.

This paper introduces a model of the new psychological contract. The employment relationship or psychological contract phenomenon is receiving considerable attention from organization development researchers and practitioners. The model aligns the changing needs of individual and organizations around eight values: Flexible Deployment, Customer-focus, Performance-focus, Project-based Work, Human Spirit & Work, Commitment, Learning & Development, and Open Information. This model can be used to benchmark an organization shifting from a culture underpinned by the traditional employment relationship to the new employment relationship.

Subject Terms:

> Industrial relations
> Organizational change
> Organizational sociology
> Performance evaluation
> Employee orientation
> Organizational structure
> Employee selection
> Commitment (Psychology)

Baran, B. E., & Adelman, M. (2010, March). Preparing for the unthinkable: Leadership development for organizational crises. *Industry & Organizational Psychology, 3*(1), pp. 45-47.

The article focuses on leadership development for organizational crises. As stated, leadership development for organizational crises should involve vicarious learning, or learning from others who have experienced crises or narrowly avoided failure. As suggested, such leadership development should involve equipping leaders with well-practiced patterns of productive problem-solving behavior. As stated, leaders must be able to communicate quickly and effectively during crises

Subject Terms:

> Leadership
> Communication in organizations
> Crises
> Ability
> Learning
> Education

Baron, J. N., Hannan, M. T., & Burton, M. (2001). Labor pains: Change in organizational models and employee turnover in young, high-tech firms. *American Journal of Sociology, 106*(4), pp. 960.

Organizational theories, especially ecological perspectives, emphasize the disruptive effects of change. However, the mechanisms producing these effects are seldom examined explicitly. This article examines one such mechanism-employee turnover. Analyzing a sample of high-technology start-ups, we show that changes in the employment models or blueprints embraced by organizational leaders increase turnover, which in turn adversely affects subsequent organizational performance. Turnover associated with organizational change appears to be concentrated among the most senior employees, suggesting "old guard disenchantment" as the primary cause. The results are consistent with the claim of neo institutionalist scholars that founders impose cultural blueprints on nascent organizations and with the claim of organizational ecologists that altering such blueprints is disruptive and destabilizing.

Subject Terms:

Labor turnover
Employment (Economic theory)
Organizational change
Employees
Performance
High technology industries

Bate, P., Khan, R., & Pye, A. (2000). Towards a culturally sensitive approach to organization structuring: Where organization design meets organizational development. *Organization Science, 11*(2), pp. 197-211.

This article describes a holistic model of intervention geared to achieving transformational change by interweaving culture and structure through the warp and weft of leadership processes. That is, it brings together organization design and organization development by advocating a culturally sensitive approach to organization structuring. Our emphasis is on process throughout and our thesis is based on empirical evidence. We undertook a lengthy action research project (which we prefer to call "action ethnography") at a large hospital trust in England. In the process of elaborating this field study, we move from an organization which was seen to be "gridlocked" and to have "lost its steering capacity", through one which was bringing development and design together by way of pilot projects and transitional structures, to one where collective dialogue and debate finally led to some collective and sensible sense making. Exploring this relationship between culture and structure enables us to put people back into design and with them, their meanings, aspirations and assumptions. It also means that we are careful to avoid detailing specific design choices or offering organizational archetypes: this article is primarily about the process issues that surround redesign rather than organization design per se, as indeed any redesign is ultimately highly specific and context-driven. Instead, however, we articulate a four- phase change model, focusing on the delicate processes by which to reframe the culture-structure relationship, enabling an organization to move towards fundamental change.

Subject Terms:

> Organizational change
> Leadership
> Organizational sociology
> Organizational structure
> Organizational behavior
> Corporate culture
> Culture
> Industrial design
> Corporations, British

Baum, J. V. (1996). Dynamics of organizational responses to competition. *Social Forces*, *74*(4), pp. 1261-1297.

This research examines how processes of adaptation and selection operate jointly in the evolution of a population of day-care centers (DCCs) in metropolitan Toronto. We study how DCCs alter their Organizational niches, defined by productive capacities and targeted resources, in response to competition and how these changes influence their survival chances. Exhibiting little structural inertia, DCCs modified their organizational niches in response to changing competitive conditions, often without any harmful effects. Indeed, DCCs that moved to less competitive organizational niches improved their survival chances. At the same time, however, competition increased rates of DCC failure and the organizational niche changes made by DCCs did not, on average, affect either the intensity of competition they faced or their longevity. We discuss the implications of these findings, which indicate that the evolution Of the DCC population is a joint function of adaptation and selection processes.

Subject Terms:

Competition

Baumgartner, R. J. (2009). Organizational culture and leadership: Preconditions for the development of a sustainable corporation. *Sustainable Development, 17*(2), pp. 102-113.

The relationship between corporate sustainability and organizational culture seems to be underestimated within the discussion of sustainable development. The research presented in this paper is based on a case study conducted in the mining industry. The hypothesis is that ambitious corporate sustainability activities and strategies have to be embedded in the organizational culture in order to be successful. If aspects of sustainable development are not part of the mindset of leaders and members of the organization, corporate sustainability activities will not affect the core business efficiently and are more likely to fail. The model of Schein for organizational culture is used to characterize corporate sustainability strategies: introverted, extroverted, conservative and visionary strategies are distinguished. Each strategy is assessed regarding the relation and the integration in the levels of organizational culture according to the model of Schein. The model consists of three levels, i.e. artifacts, values and basic assumptions. This framework is used for a case study to identify the organizational culture of a global leading mining company.

Subject Terms:

> Strategic planning
> Sustainable development
> Industrial policy
> Environmental engineering
> Economic development -- Environmental aspects
> Enterprises resource planning

Bednar, D. H., & Dodkin, L. (2009, May). Organizational learning and the development of a network comapany. *Review of Policy Research, 23*(3), pp. 329-343.

Through use of an exploratory case study, this research examines the concepts that distinguish a networked company from other organization models. These concepts are then applied in a field case study to a networked company called the Port Arthur Remediation Team (PART). PART was formed in 1996 by an integrated petroleum company, an environmental engineering concern, and a heavy construction firm to manage the remediation of an oil refining facility. How this networked firm learned to organize, coordinate activities, attain goals, and link its operational components in a useful way are described.

Beer, M. (2001). How to develop an organization capable of sustained high performance: Embrace the drive for results-capability development paradox. *Organizational Dynamics, 29*(4), pp. 233-247.

There are two schools of thought about how to manage organizational change. The dominant one today espouses a top-down, drive-for-results change strategy that employs interventions like restructuring, layoffs and reengineering. The second, much less frequently employed, espouses the development of organizational capabilities through a slower bottoms-up, unit-by-unit, high involvement approach to change. It rejects the results-driven approach as at best inadequate and at worst injurious to the development of organizational capabilities needed for sustained high performance. Through the lens of three company cases, Scott Paper Co., Champion International Corp., and Asda, we learn that embracing the paradox represented by these opposite strategies for change can result in sustained high performance and substantially higher shareholder value than either strategy applied by itself. The paradox is not often embraced--because of the failure of CEOs to manage capital market expectations, false assumptions about the nature of organizations and the leadership of change, and the unwillingness to confront organizational and management barriers that are typically known to everyone, but are not discussible. These failures block organizational learning and the development of capabilities known to be a source of sustainable competitive advantage. To embrace the paradox of change, top management must not over promise financial results to buy time for organization development. It must require division managers to lead an organizational learning process in their organization from which they learn to lead; it must orchestrate the diffusion of learning across the company; and it must lead a similar change process in the top management unit.

Subject Terms:

Organizational change
Management
Organizational
Corporate turnarounds
Organizational structure
Organizational learning

Beer, M., & Spector, B. (1993). Organizational diagnosis: Its role in organizational learning. *Journal of Counseling & Development, 71*(6), pp. 642-650.

Diagnosis can be a process that helps organizations enhances their capacity to assess and change dysfunctional aspects of their culture and patterns of behavior as a basis for developing greater effectiveness and ensuring continuous improvement. The authors set forth a framework for understanding what can be called a "learning diagnosis" in which the diagnostic" process is part of a large-scale organizational revitalization effort. In particular, they explore how the diagnostic' intervention is affected by the diagnostic consultant, by the top management sponsors of the intervention, and by the process of collecting and acting on data. They conclude with a discussion of both the opportunities and challenges of institutionalizing the learning diagnosis process.

Subject Terms:

    Organizational learning
    Organizational behavior
    Culture
    Organization
    Counseling

Beer, M., Eisenstat, R. A., & Spector, B. (1990). Why change programs don't produce change. *Harvard Business Review*, *68*(6), pp. 158-166.

Faced with changing markets and tougher competition, more and more companies realize that to compete effectively they must transform how they function. However, while senior managers understand the necessity of change, they often misunderstand what it takes to bring it about. They assume that corporate renewal is the product of companywide change programs and that in order to transform employee behavior; they must alter a company's formal structure and systems. Both these assumptions are wrong, say these authors. Using examples drawn from their four-year study of organizational change at six large corporations, they argue that change programs are, in fact, the greatest obstacle to successful revitalization and that formal structures and systems are the last thing a company should change, not the first. The most successful change efforts begin at the periphery of a corporation, in a single plant or division. General Managers, not the CEO or corporate staff people, lead such efforts. Moreover, these general managers concentrate not on changing formal structures and systems but on creating ad hoc organizational arrangements to solve concrete business problems. This focuses energy for change on the work itself, not on abstractions such as "participation" or "culture." Once general managers understand the importance of this grass-roots approach to change, they do not have to wait for senior management to start a process of corporate renewal. The authors describe a six-step change process they call the "critical path." INSETS: Tracking corporate change; contrasting assumptions about change.

Subject Terms:

Organizational change
Management
Change management
Critical path analysis
Decentralization in management
Organizational structure
Employee empowerment
Management research
Corporate reorganizations
Core & Periphery (Socioeconomic theory)
Change agents

Belassi, W., Kondra, A. Z., & Tukel, O. I. (2007, Dec). New product development projects: The effects of organizational culture. *Project Management Journal, 38*(4), pp. 12-24.

Despite the increasing use of project management within organizations, an attendant poor rate of success among these projects has been observed (Clancy & Stone, 2005; Ives, 2005). Seventy-five percent of all business transformation projects fail (Collyer, 2000) and only 16% of U.S. IT projects are completed on time and on budget (Peled, 2000). In an attempt to overcome such a high project failure rate, this paper investigates the effects of organizational culture on the performance of particular types of projects: new product development (NPD) projects. Using data from 95 U.S. organizations, the study provides evidence of the significant effects of organizational culture on NPD projects.

Subject Terms:

> Business planning
> Product management
> New products
> Project management
> Corporate culture
> Consumer goods
> Manufacturing industries
> Industrial management

Author-Supplied Keywords:

> New product development projects
> Organizational culture
> Project management
> Projects

Bennett, J., & Bush, M. (2009). Coaching in organizations. *OD Practitioner*, *41*(1), pp. 2-7.

The article discusses current trends and future opportunities in organizational coaching. It specifically refers to a study on organizational coaching, which identifies five leading trends for organizational coaching in the U.S. The trends show that coaching is evolving as a discipline and a profession and the demand for coaching is increasing. There is a move toward evidence-based coaching. Coaches have new technologies at their disposal to deliver coaching. Many organizations are implementing virtual coaching which is done entirely over the phone or Internet.

Subject Terms:

Mentoring in business
Employee – Coaching of
Internet
Technology
Business networks
Organizational change
Organizational behavior
Organization

Bercovitz, J., & Feldman, M. (2008, Jan/Feb). Academic enterpreneurs: Organizational change at the industrial level. *Organization Science, 19*(1), pp. 69-89.

This study explores the process of organizational change by examining localized social learning in organizational sub-units. Specifically, we examine participation in university technology transfer, a new organizational initiative, by tracking 1,780 faculty members, examining their backgrounds and work environments, and following their engagement with academic entrepreneurship. We find that individual adoption of the new initiative may be either substantive or symbolic. Our results suggest that individual attributes, while important, are conditioned by the local work environment. In terms of personal attributes, individuals are more likely to participate if they trained at institutions that had accepted the new initiative and been active in technology transfer. In addition, we find that the longer the time that had elapsed since graduate training, the less likely the individual was to actively embrace the new commercialization norm. Considering the localized social environment, we find that when the chair of the department is active in technology transfer, other members of the department are also likely to participate, if only for symbolic reasons. We also find that technology transfer behavior is calibrated by the experience of those in the relevant cohort. If an individual can observe others with whom they identify engaging in the new initiative, then they are more likely to follow with substantive compliance. Finally, when individuals face dissonance, a situation where their individual training norms are not congruent with the localized social norms in their work environment, they will conform to the local norms, rather than adhering to the norms from their prior experience.

Subject Terms:

> Organizational change
> Organizational growth
> Technology transfer
> Industrial research
> Technological innovations
> Organizational learning

Bloodgood, J. M., & Morrow, J. L. (2003). Strategic organizational change: Exploring the roles of environmental structure, internal conscious awareness and knowledge. *Journal of Management Studies*, 40(7), pp. 1761-1782.

We argue that strategic organizational change is best viewed as a multidimensional phenomenon consisting of various degrees of environmental structure and internal conscious awareness. Moreover, by combining this conceptualization of change with a model of organizational knowledge transfer developed by Nonaka and Takeuchi (1995), we gain a better understanding of the types of change strategies that firms will pursue, the processes they should use to implement these strategies and the likely performance outcomes from these strategies. Specifically, we suggest that the levels of tacit and explicit knowledge needed to implement the new strategies are key determinants of firm performance following strategic organizational change.

Subject Terms:

    Organizational change
    Strategic planning
    Environmental management
    Knowledge management
    Organizational structure
    Management science
    Management
    Personnel changes
    Job enrichment
    Office management
    Organization

Bloodgood, J. M., & Salisbury, D. (2001). Understanding the influance of organizational change strategies on information technology and knowledge management strategies. *Decision Support Systems, 31*, pp. 55-69.

While discussion about knowledge management often centers on how knowledge may be best codified into an explicit format for use in decision support or expert systems, some knowledge best serves the organization when it is kept in tacit form. We draw upon the resource-based view to identify how information technology can best be used during different types of strategic change. Specifically, we suggest that different change strategies focus on different combinations of tacit and explicit knowledge that make certain types of information technology more appropriate in some situations than in others.

Subject Terms:

Organizational change
Informational technology

Boonstra, J. J. (2004). *Dynamics of Organizational Change and Learning.* West Essex, England; Hoboken, N.J.: J. Wiley & Sons.

The introduction provides an overall picture of the dynamics of organizational change and learning, and the contemporary challenges that face the discipline of organizational change management. The chapter deals with the question of why many change programmes fail, and what we can do about this. It starts by discussing the insights that can be derived from theories of organizational behavior, planed change, and organizational development. New approaches to organizational change processes are elaborated. Dynamics in organizing, changing, and learning are looked upon as a source of renewal in the processes of self-organization and organizational sense making. Description of practice illustrated the theories in use. The chapter concludes with current topics that are relevant to the management of change and learning, and offers methodologies for developing practical and scientific knowledge.

Subject Terms:

> Organizational change
> Organizational learning
> Industrial management

Borges, R. (2009). Organizational change implementation and the role of human resource practices: A Brazilian case study. *Brazilian Business Review (English Edition)*, 6(3), pp. 284-295.

Although organizations are conscientious that there are many obstacles during the implementation of a strategic change, few concrete actions are carried through in this direction. With organizational change assuming a permanent characteristic in firms' routine, it is important to analyze the impact of recent changes. The objective of this paper is to investigate the relationship between human resource practices and employee's perceptions of strategic organizational change. A case study was conducted in a large Brazilian mining organization. This firm has been carrying out a strong process of organizational development in the past five years. The sample size is 234 respondents. The partial last squares (PLS) method was utilized. The results suggest that the success of a change implementation also depends on how HR practices are perceived. This is a powerful tool, which managers may utilize to minimize the negative impact of the changes. Moreover, this result confirms that HR management is strategic to organizational development, and it should participate actively in the strategy development and implementation processes.

Subject Terms:

> Case studies
> Organizational change
> Research
> Personnel management

Boss, W. R., Dunford, B. B., Boss, A. D., & McConkie, M. L. (2010). Sustainable change in the public sector: The longitudinal benefits of organization development. *Journal of Applied Behavioral Science, 46*(4), pp. 436-472.

This article examines the impact over a 30-year period of a 4-year organization development project in the Metro County Sheriff's Department. Interventions included confrontation team-building sessions, management training, process consultation, survey feedback, third-party consultation, technological interventions, implementation of methods for increasing accountability, and changes in the organization structure, the physical setting, and the policy formulation procedures. Results include improved organization climate and leader effectiveness; decreased employee turnover, jailbreaks, and citizen complaints; increased resources allocated to the organization; and improved organizational effectiveness, as measured by criminal justice leaders in the community. This research becomes the longest longitudinal study of the effects of organization development interventions in the behavioral science literature.

Subject Terms:

    Longitudinal change,
    Organization development,
    Sustainability

Bouckenooghe, D., Deyos, G., & Van den Broeck, H. (2009, Aug. 01). Organizational change questionnaire-climate of change, processes, and readiness: Development of a new instrument. *Journal of Psychology: Interdisciplinary and Applied, 143*(6), pp. 559-599.

On the basis of a step-by-step procedure (see T. R. Hinkin, 1998), the authors discuss the design and evaluation of a self-report battery (Organizational Change Questionnaire–Climate of Change, Processes, and Readiness; OCQ–C, P, R) that researchers can use to gauge the internal context or climate of change, the process factors of change, and readiness for change. The authors describe four studies used to develop a psychometrically sound 42-item assessment tool that researchers can administer in organizational settings. More than 3,000 organizational members from public and private sector organizations participated in the validation procedure of the OCQ–C, P, R. The information obtained from the analyses yielded five climate-of-change dimensions, 3 process-of-change dimensions, and three readiness-for-change dimensions.

Subject Terms:

    Organizational change
    Public sector
    Private sector
    Preparedness
    Psychometrics

Bousquet, M. (2008). Battling for hearts and minds: Organizational change as culture war. *Acedemic Bulletin of the AAUP, 94*(6), pp. 26-28.

The article focuses on the organizational culture of higher education. Most studies of organizational culture in higher education consider the rise, through the 1960s, of the increasingly distinct cultures of faculty, student and administration. These studies have focused primarily on student and faculty cultures. However, the conditions that supported the flourishing of those cultures no longer exist. The increasing economic segmentation of higher education, and the long period of political reaction that began around 1980, have diminished any sense of a vital student culture. The culture of campus administrations, on the other hand, has become ever more internally consistent and cohesive.

Subject Terms:

    Corporate culture

Bowe, C., Lahey, L., Kegan, R., & Armstrong, E. (2003). Questioning the 'big assumptions'. Part II: recognizing organizational contradictions that impede institutional change. *Medical Education, 37*(8), pp. 723-733.

Well-designed medical curriculum reforms can fall short of their primary objectives during implementation when unanticipated or unaddressed organizational resistance surfaces. This typically occurs if the agents for change ignore faculty concerns during the planning stage or when the provision of essential institutional safeguards to support new behaviors is neglected. Disappointing outcomes in curriculum reforms then result in the perpetuation of or reversion to the Status quo despite the loftiest of goals. Institutional resistance to change, much like that observed during personal development, does not necessarily indicate a communal lack of commitment to the organization's newly stated goals. It may reflect the existence of competing organizational objectives that must be addressed before substantive advances in a new direction can be accomplished. The authors describe how the Big Assumptions process (see previous article) was adapted and applied at the institutional level during a school of medicine's curriculum reform. Reform leaders encouraged faculty participants to articulate their reservations about considered changes to provide insights into the organization's competing commitments. The line of discussion provided an opportunity for faculty to appreciate the gridlock that existed until appropriate test of the school's long held Big Assumptions could be conducted. The "Big Assumptions" process proved; it is useful in moving faculty groups to recognize and questioning the validity of unchallenged institutional beliefs that were likely to undermine efforts toward change. The process also allowed the organization to put essential institutional safeguards in place that ultimately insured that substantive reforms could be sustained.

Boyne, G. A., & Meier, K. J. (2009). Environmental change, human resources and organizational turnaround. *Journal of Management Studies*, *46*(5), pp. 835-863.

Research on turnaround has largely focused on the impact of retrenchment and repositioning, and has paid less attention to the impact of changes in the task environment and human resources on recovery from decline. Moreover, all of the empirical research on turnaround has been conducted on private organizations. We develop a new model that is derived from theories of environmental and human resource effects on organizational performance. We apply this model to failing school districts in Texas, and find that turnaround is influenced by changes in the munificence and complexity of task environments, and the appointment of a new chief executive and front-line staff.

Subject Terms:

> Corporate turnarounds
> Personnel management
> Market repositioning
> Chief executive officers
> Organizational change
> Business failures
> Multivariate analysis
> Downsizing of organizations
> Guassin distribution
> Empirical research
> Performance
> School districts
> Literature reviews

Branson, C. M. (2008). Achieving organizational change through values alignment. *Journal of Educational Administration, 46*(3), pp. 376-395.

The purpose of this paper is to, first, establish the interdependency between the successful achievement of organizational change and the attainment of value alignment within an organization's culture and then, second, to describe an effective means for attaining such value alignment. Literature from the fields of organizational change, organizational culture, philosophy, psychology, and values theory is reviewed in order to develop and test the hypothesis that successful organizational change can only occur when those affected by the change are able to willingly commit to an agreed set of values aligned with the accomplishment of the organization's new outcomes. The paper then presents and reports on a trial of a simple and effective framework for achieving such value alignment in an organization. This paper supports the view that the currently acknowledged widespread resistance to organizational change is caused by a failure of current organizational change strategies to attend to a values alignment process for all those people affected by the desired change. Moreover, this paper proposes that value alignment may not just be an important integral part of organizational change strategies; it could well be the bedrock, the foundation, on which all truly successful organizational change depends. The value alignment process presented in this paper provides a very effective and efficient means for enabling people to discern, discuss, and actively support those values that will help the organization to make desired change. In essence, this process enables the alignment between personal and organizational values to occur and, thereby, allowing the organization to evolve and remain viable. The paper provides a unique perspective on the important process of value alignment within any truly successful organizational change strategy.

Subject Terms:

> Values
> Studies
> Strategic management
> Organizational change

Brasher, H. (2011). Developing interests: Organizational change and the politics of advocacy. *Journal of Politics*, *73*(4), pp. 1287-1288.

The article reviews the book "Developing Interests: Organizational Change and the Politics of Advocacy," by McGee Young

Subject Terms:

Organizational change
Books – Reviews
Nonfiction

Bright, D. S. (2009). Appreciative inquiry and positive organizational scholarship: A philosophy of practice for turbulent times. *OD Practitioner*, *41*(3), pp. 2-7.

The article discusses the relevance and being a power tool of appreciative inquiry in creating more sustainable organizations during turbulent times. It mentions that if properly understood, appreciative inquiry is a philosophy as well as practice that put a power to good use creating the condition for generativity in organizational life. Moreover, it asserts that appreciative inquiry is always an option in creating a stronger and more sustainable organization and notes that it cane understood as principle based approach to organizational changes.

Subject Terms:

> Organization
> Management
> Appreciative inquiry
> Communication in organizations
> Organizational change
> Change management
> Public administration
> Associations, institutions, etc.
> Philosophy
> Learning & scholarship
> Social aspects

Brown, L. (1992). Normative conflict management theories: Past, present, and future. *Journal of Organizational Behavior, 13*(3), pp. 303-309.

The article discusses the key characteristics of the "normative models of conflict," and how these have been affected by subsequent work, present trends and the demand made by social and organizational dynamics on conflict management. The expected responses of organizational behavior, organizational development and industrial relations to social changes are discussed, given the pattern of change and stability in social science. Global trends that contribute to the need for conflict management theory and the increase in the importance of social conflict are discussed.

Subject Terms:

Conflict management
Management
Negotiation
Crisis management
Organizational behavior
Organizational change
Social conflict
Social sciences
Dispute resolution (Law)

Browning, B., & Boys, S. (2012). Extending the conversation. *OD Practitioner*, *44*(1), pp. 18-23.

The article examines the relationship between organizational success, culture change, and interim leadership. It notes that an organization's success is associated with the existence of a strong organizational culture which can be created, imported, and managed and is considered as an achievement in managerial communication. It mentions that leadership is at the forefront of reengineering efforts for any organization that facilitates organizational culture change.

Subject Terms:

>Success in business
>Organizational change
>Leadership
>Communication in management
>Achievement

Bry, N. (2011). Social innovation? Let's start living innovations as a collective adventure. *International Journal of Organizational Innovation*, *4*(2), pp. 5-14.

After a short analysis of some reasons why teamwork is not effective, this article describes a way to optimize collective achievement along the innovation process, and complete « a whole greater than the sum of the parts ». Belief, People, Framework, Trust, and Leadership are the five landmarks that boost innovation team deliverables. Once the team operates collectively, it is then time for opening your innovation process to a social cooperation, harnessing collective intelligence more widely.

Subject Terms:

    Organizational change
    Teams in the workplace
    Leadership
    Cooperation
    Social aspects
    Swarm intelligence

Buchanan, D., & Dawson, P. (2007). Discourse and audience: Organizational change as multi-story process. *Journal of Management Studies, 44*(5), pp. 669-686.

This article is critical of monological research accounts that fail to accommodate polyvocal narratives of organizational change, calling for more fully informed case studies that combine elements of a narrative approach with processual/contextual analysis. We illustrate how contrasting versions of the same change event by different stakeholders and by the same stakeholder for different audiences, raise theoretical and methodological issues in the analysis and presentation of data on organizational change. Our argument is that research narratives (that seek to develop understanding of change processes) are necessarily selective and sieved through particular discourses that represent different ways of engaging in research. They are authored in a particular genre and written to influence target audiences who become active co-creators of meaning. Organizational change viewed from this perspective is a multi-story process, in which theoretical accounts and guides to practice are authored consistent with pre-selected narrative styles. These, in turn, are purposefully chosen to influence target audiences, but this subjective crafting is often hidden behind a cloak of putative objectivity in the written and oral presentations of academic research findings.

Subject Terms:

    Research
    Case studies
    Data analysis
    Organizational change
    Capitalists & financiers
    Audiences

Burke, W. W. (2008). *Organization Change: Theory and Practice* (2nd ed.). Los Angeles, CA: Sage Publications.

This text provides an overview of the theoretical and research foundation for our current understanding of organization change including the types of change organizations experience.

Burke, W. W. (2011). Who is the client? A different perspective. *OD Practitioner*, *43*(3), pp. 44-49.

The article offers the author's insights on the client in organization development (OD) practice. The author notes that the client is defined as the relationships and interfaces between people and units rather than individuals and units in an organization. The author cites that the importance of relationships and interfaces consider managing subordinate relationships. The author states various dilemmas of managing unit interfaces including turnover, fixed decision, and too much team spirit.

Subject Terms:

Clients
Organizational change
Industrial relations
Labor turnover
Decisions making
Teams in the workplace

Burke, W. W. (2011, Jun.). A Perspective on the field of organization development and change: The Zeigarnik effect. *Journal of Applied Behavioral Science, 47*(2), pp. 143-167.

Essentially, and perhaps arguably, there has been no innovation in the social technology of organization development (OD) since appreciative inquiry originated in 1987. It is as if the creative work of OD is done. Moreover, it is as if the mission of OD—to loosen tightly coupled systems, think large bureaucracies—has largely been achieved. Decentralization, involvement, and autonomy on the job are commonplace in many organizations. There is a paradox, however. The need for expertise in organization change has never been greater, and OD has so much to contribute, yet the failure rate for organization change efforts is around 70%, and for mergers and acquisitions, the failure rate is even larger. The premise of this article is that there is much work yet to be done. We who identify ourselves with the field of OD have unfinished business. As research on the Zeigarnik effect showed, we tend to remember things undone more than we remember things that have been completed. A purpose of this article is to create a Zeigarnik effect. Four domains of unfinished business in the field are identified and explored. There are no doubt many other domains, but these four definitely need attention. We need to know much more than we now know about how to (a) work with loosely coupled systems, (b) change the culture of an organization, (c) identify and deal with perceived resistance to change more effectively, and (d) get leadership development right—it is not about training.

Subject Terms:

> Organization development and change
> Loosely coupled systems
> Culture change
> Resistance
> Leadership development

Burnes, B. (2004). Kurt Lewin and the planned approach to change: A re-appraisal. *Journal of Management Studies, 41*(2), pp. 977-1002.

The work of Kurt Lewin dominated the theory and practice of change management for over 40 years. However, in the past 20 years, Lewin's approach to change, particularly the 3-steps model, has attracted major criticisms. The key ones are that this work: assumed organizations operate in a stable state; was only suitable for small-scale change projects; ignored organizational power and politics; and was top-down and management–driven. This article seeks to re-appraise Lewin's work and challenge the validity of these views. It begins to describe by describing Levin's background and beliefs, especially his commitments to resolving social conflict. The article then moves on to examine the main elements of his planned approach to change: Field Theory; Group Dynamics; Action Research; and the 3-Step model. This is followed by a brief summary of the major developments in the field of organizational change since Lewin's death, which, in turn, leads to an examination of the main criticisms leveled at Lewin's work. The article concludes by arguing that rather than being outdated or redundant, Lewin's approach is still relevant to the modern world.

Subject Terms:

      Organizational change
      Management
      Organizational power
      Organizational behavior
      Chance management
      Criticism
      Social conflict
      Relevance
      Field theory (Social psychology)
      Social groups
      Action research

Burton, T. T. (2011). Improve "HOW YOU" improve. *Industrial Engineer: IE, 43*(8), pp. 48-53.

The article offers information regarding strategic improvement related to industrial engineering. It discusses several factors affecting the improvement initiatives in the industry such as the lean Six Sigma including the application of obsolete improvement models, the implication of short-term financial measurements, and the non-value added improvement initiatives. It explores several frameworks of Improvement Excellence model such as one on the significance of permanent and sustainable infrastructure. It states that information technology (IT) is one of the drivers for the success of lean Six Sigma and strategic improvement initiative.

Subject Terms:

       Lean manufacturing
       Strategic planning
       Business development
       Business models
       Industrial engineering
       Information technology
       Organizational change
       Project management
       Industrial management
       Six sigma (Quality control standard)

Bushe, G. R., & Marshak, R. J. (2009). Revisioning organization development. *Journal of Applied Behavioral Science, 45*(3), pp. 348-368.

This article identifies a bifurcation in the practice of organization development (OD) that is not fully acknowledged or discussed in OD textbooks or journal articles. Forms of OD practice exist that do not adhere to key assumptions and prescriptions of the founders of OD. Some of these dialogical forms of organization development practice are described and contrasts and similarities with the original, diagnostic, form of OD are analyzed. Practices that define dialogical forms of OD are identified with a call for increased acknowledgment of this bifurcation in OD research, practice, and teaching.

Subject Terms:

    Organization development
    Change theory
    Social construction

Cady, S. H., & Fleshman, K. J. (2012). Amazing change. *OD Practitioner*, *44*(1), pp. 4-10.

The article presents the various findings from interviews with expert practitioners who were the contributors to the success of Whole System Collaboration and Change (WSCC) methods. It mentions a model that describes the characteristics of success and the driving forces to this success. It explores a research study concerning various experiences that affirms the already known aspects in the field of organizational change while attempts to stage for more practical exploration.

Subject Terms:

    Interviews
    Specialists
    Success in business
    Organizational change
    Experience

Caldwell, S. D., Herold, D. M., & Fedor, D. B. (2004). Toward an understanding of the relationships among organizational change, individual differences, and changes in person-environment fit: A cross-level study. *Journal of Applied Psychology*, *89*(5), pp. 868-882.

Organizational behavior literature has not typically viewed person-environment (P-E) fit as an outcome of change. Whereas the study of antecedents to employees' fit with their work environment has largely been restricted to the selection and socialization of newcomers, this study examines individuals' perceptions of changes in P-E fit in relation to organizational changes occurring in 34 different organizational work units. Results suggest that the relationships between organizational change and perceived changes in fit are best understood as interactions between the characteristics of the change process, the extent of change, and individual differences. Both age and mastery orientation related to perceived changes in P-E fit through interactions with aspects of the change process.

Subject Terms:

    Organizational behavior
    Organizational change
    Work environment
    Industrial psychology
    Socialization
    Adaptability (Psychology)
    Individual differences

Calendar of Events. (2010). *Organization Development Journal*, *28*(1), pp. 113.

A calendar of events related to organizational development (OD) is presented; including the 39th Annual Information Exchange on "What Is New in Organization Development and HRD" to be held during May 18-21, 2010, at the Brookley Center on Mobile Bay, Mobile, Alabama. Also includes the International Conference on Teaching and Leadership Excellence, to be held during May 30-June 2, 2010, in Austin, Texas; and OD Network Conference 2010, to be held during October 17-20, 2010, in New Orleans, Louisiana.

Subject Terms:
Organization change
Conferences & conventions
Leadership
Calendars
Teaching

Cangemi, J., Davis, R., & Lott, J. (2011). Three levels of organizational challenges and change: Needed-three different styles of leadership. *Organization Development Journal, 29*(1), pp. 27-32.

The four authors of this article decided after years of working with and observing the leaders of organizations going through various phases/stages in their organizations' life cycles, and changing --or being changed - with each phase/stage, three consistent patterns of behavior (stages) seemed to emerge. Leaders usually were changed with each stage. The stages are Survival Stage, Stability Stage, and Creative-Competitive Stage. The three stages are discussed in this article.

Subject Terms:

     Leadership
     Organizational change
     Industrial management
     Executive ability (Management)
     Success in business
     Competition (Economics)

Carlsen, A. (2006). Organizational becoming as dialogic imagination of practice: The case of the "Indomitable Gauls." *Organization Science, 17*(1), pp. 132-149.

This paper explores the relationship between authoring of identities and organizational development through a case study of the 18-year history of a professional service firm. Drawing from process theory, narrative psychology, and practice approaches to identity; I outline a perspective on organizational becoming as dialogic imagination of practice. Conceived as such, authoring takes place as a continuous stream of suggestions of what practice is, has been, and could be, and simultaneously addressing life enrichment and organizational development. Three forms of imagination of practice are identified as central in the development of the case organization: (1) the instantiating of project experiences as identity exemplars; (2) a powerful dramatizing of trajectories of practice, exemplified by use of the metaphor of the "Indomitable Gauls;" and (3) a subsequent reframing instigated by discontinuous changes in dominant activity sets. The three authoring forms are discussed in relation to organizational development and adaptation. Implications include increased attention to forward-looking authoring motives and hope, a reformulation of the identity question from "who are we?" to "what are we doing?" and a possible location of practices as belonging to stories beyond that of the organization.

Subject Terms:

> Organizational change
> Organizational behavior
> Business enterprises
> Organizational structure
> Reengineering (Management)

Carmeli, A., Gilat, G., & Waldman, D. A. (2007). The role of perceived organizational performance in organizational identification, adjustment and job performance. *Journal of Management Studies, 44*(4), pp. 972-992.

Favorable organizational status and prestige has a substantial role in shaping constituents' attitudes and actions. The status and prestige of an organization is often a reflection of its achievements or performance. In the present study, we investigate the role of organizational performance or achievement (as assessed by organizational members) in evoking employees' identification, adjustment, and job performance. The results of this study indicate that two forms of organizational performance (labeled as perceived social responsibility and development and perceived market and financial performance) are associated with organizational identification. However, when compared to perceived market and financial performance, perceived social responsibility and development had a larger effect on organizational identification, which in turn resulted in enhanced employees' work outcomes – adjustment and job performance.

Subject Terms:

    Organizational sociology research
    Employee loyalty
    Job satisfaction
    Research
    Job performance
    Employees -- Attitudes
    Economic value added
    Reputation (Sociology)

Carr, A. S., Kariyawasam, A., & Casil, M. (2008). A study of the organizational characteristics of successful cooperatives. *Organization Development Journal, 26*(1), pp. 79-87.

Market power theory suggests that greater market power can be achieved by means of a cooperative strategy that involves collaborating among firms. Although there is a vast amount of literature about the management of corporations, little has been published on the subject of managing cooperatives. In this era of increased emphasis on cost control, many organizations are finding value in joining a cooperative organization, and organizational development practitioners may find this study instructive. It discusses cooperatives in five industries and success factors apparent in these cooperatives.

Subject Terms:

> Organizational change
> Industrial efficiency
> Success in business
> Industrial management
> Organizational behavior
> Market power
> Organizational effectiveness
> Performance standards
> Corporate culture

Carrigan, M. D. (2010, April). Economic uncertanty and the role of organizational development. *Journal of Business & Economics Research, 8*(4), pp. 99-104.

The US Economy has entered an era of economic uncertainty. Stock markets are down. Unemployment is up. This paper examines the effect of economic uncertainty on organizational behavior.

Subject Terms:

    Mathematical models
    Economics
    Stock exchanges
    Securities markets
    Unemployment
    Organizational behavior

Casile, M., Hoover, K. F., & Carr, A. S. (2006). Building strength from within: How one not-for-profit asserted control? *Organization Development Journal, 24*(2), pp. 69-82.

This case study follows the evolution of a supportive housing corporation in Lucas County, Ohio from its inception as a virtual organization through a series of internal sourcing changes, each involving greater development of capabilities in-house. Skills developed in-house eventually reached a critical mass that enabled the organization to radically expand its mission and develop a strong internal culture to support its new competencies. The findings suggest that an activity that is non-core at one point in time may become an integral part of core activity in the future.

Subject Terms:

    Organizational research
    Organizational change
    Capitalism
    Financial performance

Catteeuw, F., Flynn, E., & Vonderhorst, J. (2007). Employee engagement: Boosting productivity in turbulent times. *Organization Development Journal*, *25*(2), pp. 151-157.

Like most companies in the healthcare industry, Johnson & Johnson Pharmaceutical Research & Development, L.L.C. (J&JPRD) faces the commensurate challenges of growing its business in an increasingly competitive marketplace while discovering and developing innovative new medicines. Understanding that internal and external change impacts productivity, J&J PRD's Global Organizational Development (OD) team identified employee engagement as an important tool to ensure long-term growth and success.

Subject Terms:

> Employees
> Labor productivity
> Health care industry
> Organizational change
> Marketing
> Marketing cooperatives
> Marketing models
> Research
> Marketplaces

Clark, E., & Soulsby, A. (2007). Understanding top management and organizational change through demographic and processual analysis. *Journal of Management Studies*, *44*(6), pp. 932-954.

Top management theory has been strongly influenced by demographic studies of top management teams (TMTs), but not by research into organizational adaptation to conditions of extreme institutional turbulence. This article analyses the transformation of a post-socialist enterprise through a combination of demographic and processual methods to develop an enriched account of the micro-processes through which top management constructed organizational change. Adding layers of narrative data and processual explanation directly addresses the well-rehearsed problems in demographic TMT studies. From the findings, we propose a set of theoretical arguments that conceptualizes top management in terms of management regimes, to which TMTs are politically tied and through which they seek to realize their values and strategies in organizational outcomes.

Subject Terms:

Management science -- Research
Organizational change
Research
Strategic planning
Personnel changes
Executives
Executive succession
Social aspects

Coghlan, D. (1994). Organizational development through interlevel dynamics. *International Journal of Organizational Analysis (1993 - 2002), 2*(3), pp. 264.

The article introduces the notion of organizational levels in organizational behavior. It is mentioning function of interteam relationships; identification of organizational change through individual self-development; and performance of job design.

Subject Terms:

Organizational behavior
Self-culture

Coleman, M. (2009). Self-reflection and the OD Practitioner. *OD Practitioner*, *41*(2), pp. 25-29.

A personal narrative is presented which explores the author's experience and learnings being an organization development (OD) practitioner in the U.S.

Subject Terms:

    Organizational behavior

Conbere, J., & Heorhiadi, A. (2011). Socio-economic approach to management. *OD Practitioner, 43*(1), pp. 6-10.

The article offers information on the movement Socio-Economic Approach to Management (SEAM), which started in 1973. It says that SEAM is an approach used in organizational change that considers people and finances in its analysis. SEAM shows that poor productivity of an employee is caused by poor management. Furthermore, it mentions the core values of SEAM, which are aligned with organizational development (OD) such as respecting, and valuing of every person in the organization.

Subject Terms:

> Management
> Organizational change
> Labor productivity
> Associations, institutions, etc.
> Social aspects
> Respect

Conceição, S. O., & Altman, B. A. (2011). Training and development process and organizational culture change. *Organization Development Journal, 29*(1), pp. 33-43.

This paper presents a case study, which examines the connections between the training and development process and organizational culture change in an information technology (IT) division. These take place within a higher education institution in the U.S. Findings suggest that the training and development process within the IT division served as a bridge to organizational culture change, from an old organizational culture ("legacy") to a new organizational culture ("a holistic quilt"). The foundation of the bridge was leadership and management.

Subject Terms:

> Corporate culture
> Technology attitudes
> Universities & colleges
> Employees -- Training of
> Leadership
> Organizational change

Cox, C. (2005). The power of the question: Is OD dead? *Organization Development Journal*, *23*(1), pp. 73-80.

This essay examines the OD field's fascination with the question, "Is OD dead?" The author hypothesizes that this persistent question stems from feelings of inferiority manifesting itself in negative, deficit-based discourse. An affirmative perspective that provides a positive image for OD to move towards is called for and existing opportunities for OD's expansion and prosperity are highlighted.

Subject Terms:

> Organizational change
> Personnel management
> Management
> Industrial management
> Job enrichment
> Organizational behavior

Cox, J. W. (2009). Safe talk: Revisioning, repositioning, or representing organization developmenet? *Journal of Applied Behavioral Science, 45*(3), pp. 375-377.

In this article, the author comments on the issue about the revisioning organization development suggested by authors Gervase R. Bushe and Robert J. Marshak. The author stresses that Bushe and Marshak are offering a new way of thinking regarding contemporary developments without upsetting the applecart. The author also believes the revising OD can be a helpful articulation.

Subject Terms:

> Organizational change
> Organizational behavior
> Organization

Daewoo, P., Chinta, R., Lee, M., Turner, J., & Kilbourne, L. (2011). Macro-fit versus micro-fit of the organization with its environment: Implications for strategic leadership. *International Journal of Management*, *28*(2), pp. 488-492.

As a tool to better respond to the diverse challenges facing the global business world, the concept of fit has received much attention from many management scholars and practitioners. Based on those earlier and current works on fit, we would like to advance the implications of fit for business strategy and organizational performance. In particular, strategic leadership and its role in formulating and implementing the fit (both bivariate and multivariate fit) would be a major theme of this research.

Subject Terms:

International business enterprises
Leadership
Strategic planning
Business planning
Organization
Management
Organizational effectiveness
Business development

Daif, K., & Yusof, N. (2011). Change in higher learning institutions: Lecturers' commitment to organizational change (C2C). *International Journal of Business & Social Science, 2*(21), pp. 182-194.

Organizational commitment has been identified as one of the factors determining the success or failure of any organization. However, empirical research has been lacking in scope when looking at the commitment to organizational change parameters and variables. This study specifically focuses on the world of academia in Malaysian context in order to contemplate the relationship between strategy importance (S.I), Fit of the change with strategic vision (F.V) and Job motivation (J.M) as independent variables, and commitment to change (C2C) as dependent variable. Survey was employed. The number of respondent who participated was 175. Multiple regressions were conducted to examine the relationships between the variables. The results of the study showed that strategy importance (S.I), Fit of the change with strategy vision (F.V), and job motivation (J.M) were important in obtaining lecturers commitment to change with a difference of importance for each of C2C Organizational commitment has been identified as one of the factors determining the success or failure of any organization. However, empirical research has been lacking in scope when looking at the commitment to organizational change parameters and variables. This study specifically focuses on the world of academia in Malaysian context in order to contemplate the relationship between strategy importance (S.I), Fit of the change with strategic vision (F.V) and Job motivation (J.M) as independent variables, and commitment to change (C2C) as dependent variable. Survey was employed. The number of respondent who participated was 175. Multiple regressions were conducted to examine the relationships between the variables. The results of the study showed that strategy importance (S.I), Fit of the change with strategy vision (F.V), and job motivation (J.M) were important in obtaining lecturers commitment to change with a difference of importance for each of C2C's dimensions from one to another. The results offer insights for managers and identify opportunities for future empirical research on change initiatives in organizations, especially in academic context. s dimensions from one to another. The results offer insights for managers and identify opportunities for future empirical research on change initiatives in organizations, especially in academic context.

Subject Terms:

    Organizational commitment
    Research
    Organizational change
    Change
    Empirical research
    Higher education -- Social aspects
    Social aspects

Dannemiller, K. (2004). The passing of an OD pioneer and legend. *Organization Development Journal, 22*(1), pp. 114-115.

This article presents a tribute to Kathleen Douglas Dannemiller, a contributor to the field of organization development (OD), who died of complications following emergency surgery. He was a supporter of folk music; purpose in founding the Ark; and organizational affiliations.

Subject Terms:

    Organizational behavior
    Corporate culture
    Organizational change
    Management

Darling, J. R. (2009, Summer). Organization development in an era of socioeconomic change: A focus on the key to successful management leadership. *Organizational Development Journal, 27*(2), pp. 9-26.

The current United States socioeconomic system is in a state of turmoil unlike any in recorded history, thereby calling for adjustments of major importance for the meaningful development of organizations. In responding to this development need, managerial leaders must give increased attention to the choices they make, and the most important choice for their success will be The Key. The Key is embodied in the managerial leaders' attitudes, and the commensurate thoughts and feelings communicated (vibrated) to the universe, both inside and outside of their organizations. In addition, to generate the organizational development that is necessary in an era of socioeconomic change, a commitment to organizational excellence, and the leadership strategies and values that are of primary importance to the achievement of that excellence must be a major focus. This treatise is a focus on the nature of The Key and its importance for successful management leadership of organizational development. It also introduces the four primary elements for excellence in successful organizational development: committed people, care of customers, constant innovation, and management leadership. In addition, the major leadership strategies that facilitate organizational excellence in an era of socioeconomic change (attention through vision, meaning through communication, trust through positioning and confidence through respect) are described; and the leadership values (joy, hope, charity and peace) that are important for strategic success in the achievement of excellence are discussed.

Subject Terms:

> Organizational change
> Leadership
> Organizational growth
> Development leadership
> Change management
> Organizational commitment
> Socioeconomics
> Management science
> Organizational research

Darling, J. R., & Beebe, S. A. (2007). Effective entrepreneurial communication in organization development: Achieving excellence based on leadership strategies and values. *Organization Development Journal, 25*(1), pp. 76-93.

Effective communication is a primary means whereby entrepreneurs achieve the desired levels of excellence in the development of their organizations. Research suggests that the major reflections of excellence in entrepreneurial organizations focus primarily on the care of customers, constant innovation, committed people and managerial leadership. The keys to achieving acceptable levels of excellence involve four key entrepreneurial leadership strategies: attention through vision, meaning through communication, trust through positioning and confidence through respect. Research also suggests that at the heart of successful entrepreneurial management, leadership strategies must be communication-based upon key values and a concern for people that provide the foundational core and a paradigm of interactive cues for the fulfillment of those strategies.

Subject Terms:

> Organizational change
> Organization
> Management
> Leadership
> Businessmen
> Performance standards
> Strategic planning

Darling, J. R., & Heller, V. L. (2011). The key for effective stress management: Importance of responsive leadership in organizational development. *Organization Development Journal, 29*(1), pp. 9-26.

With the current environmental turmoil that is forcing rather dramatic organizational changes today, stress has become a particularly important issue with which responsive leaders are being called upon to deal. The purpose of the present treatise is to address the nature of stress, the causes of stress, the importance of The Key for effective leadership in this undertaking---and value of The Key in contemporary organizational development. The opening analogy of the leadership perspective of Aristotle will be used in helping to focus on the need for successful leaders to "be a very great many" in the process of effective organizational stress management. The Key with which a leader communicates with employees and other individuals resides in the thoughts and feelings that are based upon his attitudes. Because potential stressful issues and events arise only when one's thoughts and feelings label them as such, The Key therefore becomes a very important element in effective stress management. The self-perception, purpose, internal power versus external force, and adaptive skills and strategies of effective leaders are also addressed. The nature of stress, stress-reducing guidelines, recognition and response to stress, and the A-B-C paradigm of stress management are dealt with as important dimensions for the responsive leadership of stress management in organizational development. Throughout the material, examples are used to illustrate more fully the importance of The Key for effective stress management by responsive organizational leaders.

Subject Terms:

> Leadership
> Organizational change
> Personnel management
> Stress management
> Adaptability (Psychology)

Decker, D., Wheeler, G. E., Johnson, J., & Parsons, R. J. (2001, Jun.). Effect of organizational change in the individual employee. *Health Care Manager, 19*(4), pp. 1-12.

Increasing market pressures force companies to implement drastic organizational changes in order to remain competitive. Budget decreases, reduction efforts, and similar changes create significant morale and job-satisfaction concerns. This study assesses the effects of budget reductions and other organizational changes on the morale of hospital employees. A survey dealing with employee perceptions of stress, workload, and performance was given to hospital employees. Not surprisingly, the survey found that morale problems resulted from the organizational changes. Employees' gender and job classification showed little significant effect on the survey results, while respondents' length of employment with the organization influenced the results slightly. The findings provide information useful for dealing with challenges of employee satisfaction, morale, and trust during times of budget limitations.

DeKlerk, M. (2007). Healing emotional trauma in organizations: An O.D.
framework and case study. *Organization Development Journal, 25*(2), pp.
49-55.

Unresolved emotional trauma in many organizations blocks peoples' capacity to be effective and ability to perform. O.D. professionals cannot eliminate suffering, but can be instrumental in influencing the healing process. O.D. programs must therefore get a new focus on facilitating the healing of emotional trauma. This article describes a theoretical and conceptual background and an O.D. framework to organizational trauma, and provides a practical case study on the healing of trauma in organizations.

Subject Terms:

> Organizational behavior
> Organizational change
> Leadership
> Case studies
> Physic trauma
> Ability
> Intellect
> Theory
> Operant behavior

Desmond, B. (2011). Effective group development. *OD Practitioner*, *43*(1), pp. 29-34.

The article discusses aspects of group development process and its efficient facilitation using a relational model, which depends on the group, maturity, and tasks. It says that the model has three phases such as connection and contacting, challenging and confrontation, and creation and commitment. It states that through action learning sessions, facilitators can enhance learning through genuine inquiries to phenomenological experiences of people, invitation of reflections, and reflexivity

Subject Terms:

      Active learning
      Facilitated learning
      Commitment (Psychology)
      Motivation (Psychology)
      Developmental psychology
      Developmental tasks
      Reflexivity

Deyos, G., Buelens, M., & Bouckenooghe, D. (2007, Dec.). Contribution of content, context, and process to understanding openness to organizational change: Two experimental simulation studies. *Journal of Social Psychology, 147*(6), pp. 607-629.

The authors examined the contribution of the content, context, and process of organizational transformation to employees' openness to change. The authors predicted that 5 factors would have a positive effect on openness to change: (a) threatening character of organizational change (content related), (b) trust in executive management (context related), (c) trust in the supervisor (context related), (d) history of change (context related), and (e) participation in the change effort (process related). The authors tested their hypotheses in 2 separate studies (N = 828 and N = 835) using an experimental simulation strategy. The first study crossed 4 variables in a completely randomized 2 x 2 x 2 x 2 factorial design. Results showed significant main effects for content, context, and process but no significant interaction effects. A second study, with a completely randomized 2 x 2 factorial design, crossed two context variables. Results showed a significant main and an interaction effect: Openness to change decreased dramatically only when history of change and trust in executive management were low

Subject Terms:

    Organizational change
    Employees-- Attitudes
    Resistance to change
    Trust
    Industrial relations
    Simulation methods

Dove, M. (1998). Conflict: process and resolution. *Nursing Management*, *29*(4), pp. 30-32.

Because most organizations function as open systems, they are susceptible to conflict. Identifying destructive conflict, seeking its root cause and using problem-solving techniques to resolve issues provide satisfactory outcomes for both sides. The steps in the conflict process and the possible solutions are given.

Subject Terms:

Conflict Management

Conflict Management -- Methods

Drori, G. S., Meyer, J. W., & Hokyu, H. (2006). *Globalization and Organization: World Society and Organization Change.* Oxford, England: Oxford University Press.

The intensification of global interdependencies and the consolidation of the global as a social horizon—both captured in the now popular term globalization—have provided fertile ground for the creation of new organizations and the expansion of existing ones. With globalization, much human activity has spawned a growing set of universalized rules and standards. The older protective armor provided by the sovereign national state and society has weakened, so much local activity become linked into the global web of organizations and institutions. In this context, both risk and opportunity are now conceived as worldwide, and forms of behavior and action are assessed in global terms. The result has been a worldwide explosion of organizations and organizing. This book provides an analysis of how and why this expansion has happened.

Dunn, J. (2006). Strategic human resources and strategic organization development: An alliance for the future? *Organization Development Journal*, *24*(4), pp. 69-76.

It is believed that it is not O.D.'s responsibility to take over the work of another functional area but to identify the cross-sections of O.D. with other disciplines (i.e., information technology, crisis management or human resources). As some have argued that the work of O.D. was created in response to the events following World War II, it is therefore only fitting that the principles of O.D. be applied to provide strategic direction to other fields, like human resources. This review highlights the evolution of the human resources field and the growing imperative of creating strategic HR operations. Specifically, this article suggests that the unique skills of O.D. practitioners in building organizational capability and demonstrating a measurable impact on workforce productivity are emerging as a primary focus of HR organizations. The practical and theoretical implications of this partnership, and the need for further study, are discussed.

Subject Terms:

Organizational change
Organizational behavior
Personnel management
Corporate governance
Crisis management
Information technology
Labor supply

Eder, P., & Marshall, E. (2010). Optimizing results through socially balanced strategies. *OD Practitioner*, *42*(3), pp. 30-35.

The article focuses on strategic planning that considers social value orientation (SVO). It emphasizes that the preferences and predisposition of individuals such as cooperation, aggression, and competition play a role in organizational structure and effectives. It offers suggestions on how executives manifest an SVO-based strategy, which include re-framing, holistic, and targeted approaches.

Subject Terms:

    Strategic planning
    Organizational effectiveness
    Business development
    Business planning
    Social values

Ehrenberg, R. H., & Stupak, R. J. (1994). Total quality management: Its relationship to administrative theory and organizational behavior and public sector. *Public Administration Quarterly*, *18*(1), pp. 75-98.

This article identifies, summarizes and evaluates research regarding theories and principles applicable to the implementation of the Total Quality Management philosophy in the U.S. New frontiers are opening for Organizational Development practitioners as experience in both the public and private sectors demonstrate the enormous potential of TQM to meet organizational challenges. This emerging evidence suggests that a new thrust of TQM encompasses and integrates many elements of organizational development and change theory. During the early twentieth century, the concept of scientific management developed by Frederick Taylor sought to increase productivity by analyzing and then standardizing each step of the production process. While workers were consulted in designing the standard or most efficient work processes, management was responsible for productivity and quality. At about the same time, Henri Fayol devised the first comprehensive theory of management. It was intended to be universally applicable to all organizations, although it required some modification when used in the public sector, which Fayol called enterprises having no monetary objectives. While he made no mention of quality or customer expectations, Fayol did recognize the importance of a planning process that includes worker participation.

Subject Terms:

> Total quality management
> Organization
> Organizational change
> Organizational structure
> Manufacturing processes
> Management science

Endres, G. M. (2008). The human resource craze: Human performance improvement and employee engagement. *Organization Development Journal*, *26*(1), pp. 69-78.

Numerous terms mean different things to different people engaged in organization development. This article helps O.D. practitioners recognize the differences regarding two such "faddish" terms, human productivity improvement (HPI) and employee engagement, and encourages researchers to more completely define such terms. By implication, it encourages practitioners to define their terms within their scope of work so that results might be more readily measured, hence more meaningful.

Subject Terms:

> Human capital
> Labor supply
> Organizational change
> Personnel management
> Organizational behavior
> Labor productivity
> Corporate culture
> Performance standards
> Employees -- Rating of
> Industrial productivity
> Engagement (Philosophy)

Engle, P. (2011). Tough transitions for survival. *Industrial Engineer: IE*, *43*(11), pp. 24.

The article offers information on various factors needed to manage organizational change. It says that a strong leadership is of primary importance, emphasizing the need for leaders' visibility and commitment during the transition in an organization. It states that staff needs to have a clear idea on what the management expects for the future. Moreover, it notes that the success of the business lies on the ability of the management to provide best value for its consumers.

Subject Terms:

    Organizational change
    Management
    Leadership
    Transition economies
    Success in business
    Consumers
    Commitment (Psychology)

Engle, P. (2012). Leaders push change to manage growth. *Industrial Engineer: IE,* *44*(2), pp. 24

The author offers opinions on the management of corporate growth. Growth is said to be essential for the survival of any business enterprise, and therefore should be the most important priority for executives. It is argued that growth of necessity creates constant organizational change, and that leadership requires recognition of the need for reinvention of the firm.

Subject Terms:

Organizational change
Management
Corporations – Growth
Business planning
Organizational growth
Organizational behavior

Erwin, D. (2009). Changing organizational performance: Examining the change process. *Hospital Topics, 87*(3), pp. 28-40.

A survey of hospital chief executive officers found financial challenges to be the most important issue facing their organizations (American College of Healthcare Executives 2007). However, researchers (Griffith et al. 2006; Langabeer 2008) have found that hospitals have been unsuccessful in significantly improving or changing their financial performance. In the present case study, the author reports how hospital leaders achieved cost reductions while maintaining quality patient care in the complex and messy reality of their organization. The author (serving as a consultant to leadership and using an action research methodology) examined the process of leading change in a hospital organization and the associated reactions of individual organizational members to change interventions. The author tried to link current theory and practice while identifying those factors most crucial to leading this financial change initiative. The major challenges faced, and what seemed most effective in addressing those challenges. The author also examined 4 phases of the change process: realizing the need to change, planning the change, implementing the change, and sustaining the change.

Subject Terms:

> Change Management
> Health Facility Administration
> Organizational Change

Esty, K. (2011). Lessons from Muhammad Yunus and the Grameen Bank. *OD Practitioner*, *43*(1), pp. 24-28.

The article offers the author's insights on the leadership and management style of Grameen Bank's managing director Muhammad Yunus. The author says that Yunus dedicates his life to end poverty, so he modeled a project that provides loans to the poor or microcredit in Bangladesh. Moreover, she lists eight key actions that she learned from Yunus on leading long-term organizational change including setting forth of an inspiring vision, challenging the prevailing wisdom, and becoming flexible.

Subject Terms:

    Bank management
    Microfinance
    Organizational change
    Transformational leadership

Ettorre, B. (1996). The handy reference to the future. (Cover story). *Management Review, 85*(7), pp. 12.

Presents an interview with organizational thinker, teacher and author Charles Handy. Belief that societies and organizations must profoundly change in order to endure; Characterizations of a federalist organization and a globalized organization; Negative effects of corporate downsizing; Ramifications of the growing technological access to information.

Faull, K., Kalliath, T., & Smith, D. (2004). Organizational culture: The dynamics of culture on organizational change within a rehabilitation center. *Organization Development Journal, 22*(1), pp. 40-55.

Discusses the dynamics of culture on organizational change within a rehabilitation center in New Zealand. Comparison of the present day culture of a rehabilitation organization with the culture developed in 1944; Commonalities and differences between present day and original cultures; Factors that have been resistant to change; Author's recommendations to leaders of the organization.

Subject Terms:

    Organizational change
    Organizational structure
    Corporate culture
    Management
    Rehabilitation centers

Fernandez, S., & Rainey, H. G. (2006, May). Managing successful organizational change in the public sector. *Public Administration Review, 66*(2), pp. 168-176.

This article discusses organizational change in public organizations. Existing research that contains various models and frameworks describes the process of implementing change within organizations and point to several factors that contribute to success. Managerial leaders must communicate the need for change and then develop a course of action or strategy for implementing the change. The leaders have to build internal support for change and reduce resistance to it. A group or individual from within the organization should support the cause for change and managerial leaders have to develop support from political overseers and key external stakeholders. Organizational resources should be redeployed toward new activities including developing a strategy for change.

Subject Terms:

    Organizational change
    Management
    Executives
    Associations, institutions, etc.
    Public institutions

Fetterhoff, T., Nila, P., & McNamee, R. C. (2011). Accessing internal knowledge:
Organizational practices that facilitate the transfer of tacit knowledge.
Research Technology Management, *54*(6), pp. 50-54.

The article discusses the results of a 2010 survey that examined how companies identify and access internal knowledge. The three primary areas of focus for the survey are organizational practices, the concept of tacit knowledge and barriers to knowledge transfer. A number of Industrial Research Institute (IRI) member companies participated in this survey. According to the survey, developing new ideas, concepts and innovations is the top strategic priority of companies for knowledge management. It also found that respondents' top tactical objectives include continuous development for high potential employees and gaining access to consumer perspectives.

Subject Terms:

    Industrial surveys
    Knowledge management
    Organizational behavior
    Innovations in business
    Human's capital
    Career development
    Customer relations
    Tacit knowledge
    Knowledge transfer (Communication)

Fincham, R. (1999, May). The consultant-client relationship: Critical perspectives on the management of organizational change. *Journal of Management Studies*, *36*(3), pp. 335-351.

The management consultancy industry is attracting more and more attention. The critical literature in particular has questioned how a non-codified body of knowledge like 'consultancy' could become so apparently influential. The answering emphasis has been on the symbolic nature of consultant strategies and consultancy as a powerful system of persuasion. However, an emerging structural perspective has developed a rather different view, focusing on the limits of the industry discourse, and the constraints of a consultancy role defined largely by external forces. While it is useful to contrast the two perspectives--strategic and structural--they can also be viewed as complementary, and indeed a number of writers have been well aware both of the importance of consultant strategies and the context of consultancy work. In particular, they have explored the interaction between consultant and client, and called attention to factors like the countervailing power of client organizations and the uncertainty of the management task. The paper aims to contribute to this debate and draws on case studies of consultants' role in the management of organizational change--one of clients with considerable market power, and another of interdependency between consultant and client. The point stressed is that the consultancy process contains no 'necessary' structures (which may be implied by pairings such as the dependent client and indispensable consultant, or alternatively the resistant client and vulnerable consultant). Instead, the consultant-client relationship is best regarded as part of an overarching managerial structure and a contingent exchange that assumes a variety of forms.

Subject Terms:

    Consultants
    Professional-client relations
    Organizational change
    Management
    Knowledge management
    Consulting firms
    Knowledge-based theory of the firm
    Contingency theory (Management)
    Theory of constraints (Management)
    Case method
    Professional-client communication

Finlay, J. S. (2008). Feedback and more feedback. *Organization Development Journal, 26*(3), pp. 5-7.

The article discusses various reports published within the issue including one on enhancing team effectiveness and another on exploring organizational change cynicism.

Subject Terms:

Teams in the workplace
Organizational change

Finlay, J. S. (2008). Letter from the editor. *Organization Development Journal,* *26*(1), pp. 5-8.

The article discusses various reports published within the issue, including the use and practice of the term engagement by organizations and the cognitive mapping and diagnostic aspects of organizational change.

Subject Terms:

Organizational change
Engagement (Philosophy)

Finlay, J. S. (2009, Summer). Letter from the editor. *Organizational Development Journal, 27*(2), pp. 5-6.

The article discusses various reports published within the issue, including one by Scott Allen on the theories of action in leadership development, one by Bridget Gilmore on organizational boundary spanning to leadership and another by William Seidman and Michael McCauley on a model for grassroots organizational development.

Finlay, J. S. (2009). Letter from the editor. *Organization Development Journal*, *27*(1), pp. 5-7.

The article discusses various reports published within the issue including "New Paradigms in Organization Development," by Fahri Karakas, "The New Employee-Employer Relationship Model," by Tim Baker, and "Understanding Large Group Intervention Processes: A Complexity Theory Perspective," by Michael Arena.

Subject Terms:

Organizational change
Industrial relations

Forman, S. J., Susan, G., Smallwood, D. L., & Nagle, R. J. (2005, May). Organizational and individual factors in bringing research to practice: What we know, where we need to go. *Psychology in the School, 42*(5), pp. 569-576.

In this commentary, we examine the articles in this special issue in terms of a continuum of research to practice strategies currently used in school psychology. On one end of the continuum is the publish/hope approach, and at the other end is the change the organization to fit the innovation approach. We present the concept of innovation implementation as central to research to practice issues, and we review literature about organizational and individual factors that affect the success of innovation implementation. A new research-to-practice approach in which there is a dynamic, ongoing alliance between researchers and practitioners is suggested. Implications for researchers, practitioners, trainers, and professional organizations are described.

Subject Terms:

    Physician practice patterns
    School psychology
    Medicine -- Research
    Organization
    Innovation adoption
    Medical personnel

Freedman, A. M. (2011). Using action learning for organization development and change. *OD Practitioner*, *43*(2), pp. 7-13.

The article demonstrates how action learning (AL) theory, methods and skills can enhance current change management efforts, particularly those in which technical consultants partner with optometrist and change practitioners. It examines how AL emphasizes the learning and development of individuals, the team and the organization. It also offers a definition of the discipline and practices of optometrists and change practitioners.

Subject Terms:

    Organizational change
    Change management
    Complex organizations
    Active learning

Freiling, J., & Fichtner, H. (2010). Organizational culture as the glue between people and organization: A competence-based view on learning and competence building. *Zeitschrift Für Personalforschung, 24*(2), pp. 152-172.

Is organizational culture a catalyst of competence development? This paper argues it is. The reason for this is that organizational culture fosters the process of learning and competence building and works as a glue between people and the organization they belong to. We employ a most recently developed approach belonging to market process theory, the so-called 'competence-based theory of the firm', to explain these causal relationships.

Subject Terms:
> Corporate culture
> Theory of the firm
> Organizational effectiveness
> Industrial relations
> Performance
> Learning

Author-Supplied Keywords:
> Competence building
> Competence-based Theory of the Firm (CbTF)

Funches, D. (2011). Come to the edge and go beyond. *OD Practitioner*, *43*(1), pp. 1-3.

The article offers the author's insights on pushing the limits in the field of organizational development (OD) and its practitioners. The author mentions the words of English poet Christopher Logue, which state to come to the edge and fly and relates the words on facing difficult challenges in order to succeed. The author states that she sees the Organization Development Network as a network of networks and adds the implications of going to the edge and flying such as the sharing of knowledge.

Subject Terms:

Organizational change
Associations, institutions, etc.
Success

Gakovic, A., & Yardley, K. (2007). Global talent management at HSBC. *Organization Development Journal, 25*(2), pp. 201-205.

Global talent management is an organizational development solution that supports the HSBC vision to be the world's leading financial services company. This article will describe how the global talent management solution aligns to our business strategy and how we developed, refined, and implemented our global process in the context of our culture and core values. We will share best practices, challenges, lessons learned, and results from implementing our integrated talent identification and development system. The unique contribution of this work is the examination of ways to address complexities involved in executing people strategy in a global, matrixed, and results-focused business environment.

Subject Terms:

Management
Organization
Leadership
Business
Organizational change
Organizational behavior
Business planning
Best practices
Standards

Gebo, E., Boyes-Watson, C., & Pinto-Wilson, S. (2010, March/April). Re-conceptualizing organizational change in the comprehensive gang model. *Journal of Criminal Justice, 38*(2), pp. 166-173.

Organizational change and development is one of the cornerstones of successful crime prevention and intervention efforts, yet it has received little empirical attention in the areas of crime and justice. This lack of empirical attention extends to the national Comprehensive Gang Model, which explicitly states that organizational change and development is a key strategy. Borrowing concepts from the management field, the authors argue that the Comprehensive Gang Model should be re-conceptualized so that organizational change and development is the foundation upon which other strategies are built. Application of this re-specified model is demonstrated through a case study in central Massachusetts utilizing learning communities as a vehicle to obtain sustainable change. Assessment of the organizational change and development is also discussed.

Gellermann, W. (2004). Organization development, corporations, and society. *Organization Development Journal, 22*(2), pp. 29-36.

This article reflects on questions organization development (OD) practitioners must consider about their work with corporations. Throughout the article the definition of OD was also mentioned by the author; as well as key concepts in thinking about OD processes.

Subject Terms:

    Organizational change
    Organizational behavior
    Organization
    Corporation

Gentry, W. A., & Leslie, J. (2007). Competencies for leadership development: What's hot and what's not when assessing leadership-implications for organization development. *Organization Development Journal*, *25*(1), pp. 37-46.

Organizations and O.D. practitioners use multisource (multi-rater or 360-degree) instruments for leadership development purposes, whereby observers (e.g., peers, subordinates, supervisors) rate and assess a person. However, many competencies can be chosen to form the multisource instrument. This paper provides a scan of which competencies organizations are using (and not using) to form their own multisource instrument for leadership development purposes, showing trends in today's workplace. Implications for organizations and O.D. practitioners are also discussed.

Subject Terms:

Organizational change
Organizational behavior
Leadership
Work environment
Employees

Georgopoulos, B. S., & Tannenbaum, A. S. (1957). A study of organizational effectiveness. *American Sociological Review*, *22*(5), pp. 534-540.

Organizational effectiveness is one of the most complex and least tackled problems in the study of social organizations. Many difficulties arise with attempts to define the concept of effectiveness adequately. Some stem from the closeness with which the concept becomes associated with the question of values (e.g., "management" versus "labor" orientations). Other problems arise when researchers choose a priori criteria of effectiveness that seem intuitively right, without trying systematically to place them within a consistent and broader framework. In effect, specific criteria that might be proper in one case may be entirely inappropriate to other organizations. The question arises whether it is possible to develop a definition of effectiveness and to derive criteria that are applicable across organizations and can be meaningfully placed within a general conceptual framework

Subject Terms:

  Organizational effectiveness
  Social structure
  Judgment
  Problem solving
  Sociology -- Research
  Organizational

Gill, J., & Whittle, S. (1993). Management by Panacea: Accounting for transience. *Journal of Management Studies, 30*(2), pp. 281-295.

The cyclical nature of much consultant-led activity designed to improve managerial effectiveness is explored through three consultant-driven approaches to organizational improvement - management by objectives, organization development and total quality management. Such packaged programmes seem to proceed through phases of high enthusiasm and much activity followed by a period of disillusionment, to be replaced by the next stage panacea. An attempt is made to offer some explanation of the transitory nature of much managerial activity which is believed to lie fundamentally in cultural and psychodynamic phenomena. Such an analysis may provide some clues to the search for remedial steps that might be taken to find more enduring ways to bring about increased managerial effectiveness in organizations, although by the very nature of our diagnosis we remain pessimistic.

Subject Terms:

> Consultants
> Industrial management
> Management by objectives
> Organizational effectiveness
> Organizational change
> Personnel management
> Total quality management
> Management research
> Organizational sociology research
> Research
> Management styles
> Corporate culture

Gilley, A., Gilley, J. W., & McMillan, H. S. (2009). Organizational change: Motivation, communication, and leadership effectiveness. *Performance Improvement Quarterly, 21*(4), pp. 75-94.

Research indicates that numerous variables have an impact on a leader's effectiveness. This study explores the behaviors associated with leadership effectiveness in driving change. The findings confirm previous research that identifies change effectiveness skills, while isolating the specific leader behaviors deemed most valuable to implementing change: motivation and communication.

Subject Terms:

> Motivation
> Communication
> Leadership
> Organizational Change
> Effectiveness studies

Gilmore, B. (2009). Decreasing organizational design failure: Organizational and leadership boundary spanning. *Organization Development Journal, 27*(2), pp. 97-105.

This paper provides an overview of the current literature regarding organizational boundary spanning, its definition as well as benefits to organizations. The second half of this paper intended to apply the same concept to leadership but found that leaders participate for different reasons. Therefore, a new concept called leadership boundary spanning is being proposed.

Subject Terms:

> Organizational effectiveness
> Organizational change
> Leadership
> Executive ability (Management)
> Development leadership
> Industrial relations
> Organizational sociology

Goldberg, M., & Jules, C. (2010). Organization development and human resources. *OD Practitioner*, *42*(4), pp. 36-39.

The article discusses the primary domains and distinctions of the organization development (OD) and human resources (HR), such as their assumptions about human beings, core ideas, and practices. It also mentions the shared characteristics of the two fields including certain key principles and skills. Practical implications on the relationship between OD and HR are further emphasized.

Subject Terms:

    Organizational behavior
    Organizational effectiveness
    Organizational change
    Personnel departments
    Personnel management
    Support services (Management)

Goldberg, R. A. (2005). Resistance to coaching. *Organization Development Journal, 23*(1), pp. 9-16.

Coaching has become a popular method to develop senior executives, yet its effectiveness is open to debate. First, coaching is often conducted without addressing the environment in which the executive operates, making gains derived from coaching difficult to sustain. Second, executives often resist being coached, inhibiting them from learning or acting differently. This article demonstrates executive coaching to be an effective management and organizational development tool, particularly when coaches become more aware of their own resistance to coaching.

Subject Terms:

> Management
> Organizational change
> Industrial management
> Business
> Executive coaching
> Coaching (Transportation)

Golembiewski, R. T. (1991). Organizational development in the Third World: values, closeness of fit and culture-boundedness. *International Journal of Human Resource Management*, 2(1), pp. 39-53.

This paper seeks to counterbalance some common arguments about the role of organizational development (OD) in Third World settings. OD is a value-laden technology and this raises issues of the closeness of fit of specific OD approaches or designs to different cultures, histories and settings. Most organizational theorists recommend a close fit, based upon an overall characterization of OD and estimates of the features of macro cultures such as nations or regions. This paper urges a more differentiated perspective, based on evidence that OD works, on balance, in a broad range of contexts. Specifically, OD designs/approaches are not homogeneous, and are neither the nation-states nor organizations in which OD is applied. The paper suggests a number of ways in which OD practitioners might become more sensitive to different contexts and thereby improve their judgments about the advisability of making OD interventions.

Subject Terms:

Organizational change
Organizational behavior
Development countries
Industrial management
Corporate culture
Technological transfer
Conflict management
Cultural values
Primacy effect (Learning)
Centrality
Success
Awareness

Golembiewski, R. T. (1994). Organizational development and change as prismatic. *International Journal of Organizational Analysis (1993 - 2002)*, 2(3), pp. 229.

This symposium seeks to contribute to an expanding core for Organizational Development and Change (ODC) in the global area. ODC is developing "prismatic" features, and these at once signal robust activity even as they threaten spin-offs. The five contributions below deal with generic measurement issues; the introduction of a Hawaiian design for conflict management; the central levels of interlevel designs and dynamics in OSC; gender proportions and their organizational covariant; and an updating of the evaluative literature on ODC applications in national settings having moderate-to-low GNP per capita.

Subject Terms:

Organizational change
Conflict management

Golembiewski, R. T. (2004). Twenty questions for our future: Challenges facing OD and ODers, or whatever it is labeled. *Organization Development Journal*, *22*(2), pp. 6-20.

The article discusses the challenges facing organization development (OD) and OD practitioners. Categories with which OD must deal in its future are classified, namely, concepts of operating realities, boundaries of application and analysis, governance via values and expanding OD field.

Subject Terms:

    Organizational change
    Organizational behavior
    Organization
    Management

Golembiewski, R. T. (2006). Building ODC as an academic discipline: Scholarship in ODC. *Organization Development Journal, 24*(3), pp. 88-89.

The article focuses on building organizational development and change as an academic discipline. The author points out two categories on organizational development and change. It includes the success rates are substantial in the case of numerous fragments of goal-based empirical theories, which guide applications to achieve clusters of intended effects and the interpretations of success rates grow.

Subject Terms:

    Organizational change
    Organizational behavior
    Organizational sociology
    Organizational structure
    Organizational commitment

Gopalakrishnan, S. C. (2010). Embracing the "Gift Story". *OD Practitioner, 42*(1), pp. 4-9.

The article focuses on the effort of the public school district in California to manage the financial crisis, giving opportunity to develop a deep organizational change. The Rowland Unified School District (RUSD) embraced the redesign process called think-tank to create innovative ways to accomplish its goal more effectively with fewer financial resources. It notes that through the redesign process, district leaders will be able to serve the community effectively, most especially to the students.

Subject Terms:

Management
School administration
Organizational change
School districts
Public schools
Community & school

Graf, T. (2009, Summer). The future of OD: Developing an effective virtual organization for the OD network. *OD Practioner, 41*(3), pp. 30-36.

The article asserts that organizational development (OD) network is well-positioned in leading growth into the virtual future. It presents the result of an organizational assessment and an implementation plan for integration new products and services for OD network. It then demonstrate that an effective virtual organization leis at the intersection of human needs, business process, strategy and vision where an organization must adapt its core to respond changing market conditions with virtual diverse workforce.

Subject Terms:

> Organization
> Management
> Associations, institutions, etc.
> Organizational change
> Business planning
> Labor supply
> Interorganizational relations
> Organizational learning
> Organizational behavior
> Social aspects
> Virtual reality

Greenwood, R., & Hingings, C. R. (1996, Oct.). Understanding radical organizational change: Bringing together the old and the new institutionalism. *The Academy of Management Review, 21*(4), pp. 1022-1054.

The complexity of political, regulatory, and technological changes confronting most organizations has made radical organizational changes from the perspective of neo-institutional theory. The principal theoretical issue addressed in the article is the interaction of organizational context and organizational action. The article examines the processes by which individual organizations retain, adopt, and discard templates for organizing, given the institutionalized nature of organizational fields.

Subject Terms:
> Organizational change
> Organizational structure
> Organizational effectiveness
> Industrial organization
> Industrial management
> Competitive advantage
> Industrial organization (Economic theory)
> Strategic planning
> Industrial efficiency
> Industrial productivity

Griffin, K. H. (2008). Metaphor, language, and organizational transformation. *Organization Development Journal, 26*(1), pp. 89-97.

The need exists to identify language that will enable leaders to address the needs of the whole person in the workplace. Being able to use such a language—especially a common language—can enable organization development practitioners and researchers to better learn from experience and one another to effectively influence positive change in organizations. Organizations most likely to succeed in the continuous white water of the marketplace will be led by individuals who recognize the importance of efforts to engage the hearts of employees at all levels as part of their strategic business planning.

Subject Terms:

> Organizational change
> Organizational effectiveness
> Corporate culture
> Business planning
> Work environment
> Industrial management
> Organizational behavior
> Personnel management
> Industrial efficiency

Griffin, M. M. (2006). Applicability of O.D. within a university setting. *Organization Development Journal, 24*(4), pp. 77-83.

This paper focuses on strategic organization development techniques and methodologies and explores whether, in fact, these concepts and principles can be applied effectively in small private colleges and universities. Larger American universities have utilized O.D. processes in a variety of contexts but there is little, if any, evidence that these techniques and methodologies can be utilized or measured in smaller educational organizations. The paper explores the basic tenets of strategic organization development. Following that, the decision-making context in smaller academic environments is explained. Whether such principles and practices can be of value at smaller academic (education not for profit) environments is discussed.

Subject Terms:

    Organizational change
    Organizational behavior
    Universities & colleges
    Schools
    Decision-making
    Problem solving
    Education

Griffin, N. (2003). Personalize your management development. *Harvard Business Review, 81*(3), pp. 113-119.

Most organizations struggle with leadership development. They promote top performers into management roles, put them through a few workshops and seminars, and then throw them to the wolves. Managers with the ability to survive and thrive are rewarded; those without it are disciplined or reassigned. The problem is, an alarming number of people fall into the second category. This happens not because managers lack skills but because companies fail to realize that there is no single kind of leader-in-training. In this article, Natalie Shope Griffin, a consultant in executive and organizational development at Nationwide Financial, describes four kinds of managers-in-training, each embodying unique challenges and opportunities. Reluctant leaders appear to have all the necessary skills to be excellent managers but cannot imagine themselves succeeding in a leadership role. Arrogant leaders have the opposite problem; they believe they already possess all the management skills they will ever need. Unknown leaders are overlooked because they do not develop relationships outside of a small circle of close colleagues. Finally, there are the workaholics who put work above all else and spend 100 hours a week in the office. The author outlines specific training approaches tailored to each type of prospective leader. By focusing on the unique circumstances of individual managers, investing in them early in their careers, offering effective coaching, and providing real-life management experiences, Nationwide's leadership-development program has produced hundreds of successful leaders.

Subject Terms:

> Leadership
> Executives -- Training of
> Workaholics
> Executive ability (Management)
> Management styles
> Occupational training
> Personnel management
> Employees -- Training of
> Career development
> Employee motivation
> Leaders

Griffith, T. L. (1999). Research in organizational change and development, vol. 10. *Administrative Science Quarterly*, *44*(1), pp. 187-188.

There is little argument that organizational change is increasingly important. Turbulent organizational environments, hyper competition, and related organizational activities demand that organizations manage change effectively (e.g., Ilinitch, D'Aveni, and Lewin, 1996). Organizations must perceive and respond to changes in their environments, independently create new environments, and learn from their experiences. This book, 'Research in Organizational Change and Development,' vol. 10, edited by William A. Pasmore and Richard W. Woodman, takes on these issues in a variety of ways.

Subject Terms:

Research
Book – Reviews

Hanna, D. (2010). Organization development and human resources management. *OD Practitioner*, *42*(4), pp. 12-16.

The article presents the author's insights on the idea of Herb Strokes, a pioneering change agent at Procter & Gamble Co., on the need to separate human resources (HR) and organization development (OD). He comments on Herb's views of traditional HR role and illustrates the apparent connections of the two forces. An HR Competency Study conducted by RBL Inc. and the University of Michigan Ross School is presented. It also lists the HR competencies such valuing diversity and taking a new role

Subject Terms:

> Personnel management
> Organizational change
> Core competencies
> Goal setting in personnel management
> Diversity in the workplace

Haroon, M., Qureshi, T., Sindhu, M., & Anjum, S. (2010). Influencing factors of product performance & organizational performance. *Interdisciplinary Journal of Contemporary Research in Business*, 2(2), pp. 487-504.

Many scholars are of the view that market orientation culture leads to superior new product performance as well as organizational performance. They say that development of new product brings immense changes in the organizational performance as well as it creates innovation in the market. However, none of them checked market orientation, new product advantage, proficiency in launching the product with competitive environment. Competitor orientation gives knowledge about the customer`s buying pattern, whether they are satisfied are not? Moreover, why do they shift to other companies? However, competitor environment is about the behavior of customers who were loyal with competitors; which companies were in competition? In addition, whether this competition is due to price between these companies or it is based on the quality of the product and services. To determine the impact on organizational performance and new product performance, we conducted this research from 26 organizations, while selecting five respondents from each one, totaling 130 questionnaire. These organizations were performing very well in the last couple of years from the food industry and beverages industry. Result shows that there is positive relation of organizational performance and new product performance with market orientation, proficiency in launch efficiency, new product advantage and competitive environment.

Subject Terms:

     Organizational behavior
     Food industry
     New products – Marketing
     Product management
     Competitor orientation
     Customer satisfaction
     Technological innovations
     Quality of products
     Quality of service
     Gross domestic product

Harrison, B., & Tarter, D. (2007). Building and sustaining a high performance internal O.D. practitioner team. *Organization Development Journal, 25*(2), pp. 187-192.

Internal organization development (O.D.) consultants can play a pivotal role in improving an organization's capability portfolio and overall competitive advantage. However, the full value of the O.D function is often not recognized by line managers and business leaders, as O.D. practitioners are often perceived as a dispensable part of an organization and become easy targets when leaders are faced with cutting costs. To overcome this perception, a team of internal O.D. experts at Raytheon Company developed and implemented an entrepreneurial model that allowed it to establish itself as a sustainable resource for line managers and business leaders. This paper provides an overview of the process and critical success factors that Raytheon O.D applied in collaborating with line managers and business leaders to improve the firm's organizational effectiveness. It offers a blueprint for how other O.D. functions can more effectively demonstrates it value and role as a strategic business partner.

Subject Terms:

Organizational change
Consultants
Investments
Competitive advantage
Marketing strategy
Business planning
Cost
Leadership
Executive ability (Management)

Harrower, N. L. (2010). Applying OD principles to non-OD projects. *OD Practitioner*, *42*(1), pp. 26-30.

The article examines a strategic consulting project on applying organization development (OD) principles to non-OD projects. It states that practitioners can increase their awareness and scope of interventions to enhance the project, team and plan by developing and integrating OD processes into business consulting projects. It adds that OD practitioners can bring out the best in employees and clients, by combining OD and business skill sets.

Subject Terms:

Organizational change
Organizational effectiveness
Employees
Clients
Business consultants
Business skills

Head, T. C. (2006). Strategic organization development: A failure of true organization development. *Organization Development Journal, 24*(4), pp. 21-28.

As we currently approach strategic organization development (the complete transformation of all systems in a coordinated fashion), there is little doubt that it represents nothing but a failure for 'traditional' organization development. This is not to say strategic efforts are not valuable or successful. Rather it means that the organization failed to use organization development to prevent the need for such drastic actions. It is time we return to our roots and redefine strategic organization development as the proactive use of the field's techniques and philosophies to identify and correct problems before they become 'life threatening.'

Subject Terms:

>   Organizational behavior
>   Organizational change
>   Organization
>   Management
>   Industrial psychology
>   Business ethics
>   Interorganizational relations

Head, T. C., & Sorensen Jr., P. F. (2005). The evaluation of organization development interventions: An empirical study. *Organization Development Journal, 23*(1), pp. 40-55.

A survey of Fortune 500 HR Executives was used to test seven hypotheses concerning the evaluation of organization development interventions. Among the findings are uncertainty in the intervention creates the client's expectation for multiple-level evaluations, and idiosyncratic investment in an intervention effects the desired level of evaluation rigor.

Subject Terms:

> Organizational change
> Management
> Organizational behavior
> Personnel management
> Executives
> Industrial management

Henry, P. K. (1997). Overcoming resistance to organizational change. *Journal of the American Diabetic Association, 97*(10), pp. 145-147.

Resistance to assertive organization change is inevitable because people are asked to reexamine and modify their behavior, which breeds resistance. Resistance serves to maintain equilibrium until the reasons for change are both conscious and compelling. Instead of accepting people's feelings as excuses, persistently push for what you know needs to happen in the face of today's harsh realities. Provide clarity, time, support, and the stability of a persistent message. J Am Diet Assoc. 1997; 97 (suppl 2):S145–S147.

Some leaders become upset with managers, physicians, and others who resist organizational change strategies, while other leaders see resistance as an indication that they may have done something wrong strategically. The fact is the resistance to assertive organizational change is inevitable because people are asked to reexamine and modify their behavior, which breeds resistance.

Who is responsible for overcoming resistance? Responsibility begins with the people who have the vision. It then becomes shared, but ultimately rests on the resister. Leaders need to take proactive and reactive steps to handle resistance.

Herzog, R. J. (1991). Ironies in organizational development (Book). *Social Science Quarterly (University Of Texas Press), 72*(2), pp. 398-399.

Golembiewski's book is a culmination of his old works and new material that unifies his main concern of improving the success of organizational development (OD) by reducing multiple ironies. I commend Golembiewski's proactive posture and devotion to improving OD theory and practice. His willingness to fix something that is not broken is an important contribution to the OD field.

The first 11 chapters address six ironies: (1) relative success but pessimism about practice; (2) relative success without a learning model; (3) relative success without differentiating people; (4) relative success without specifying contexts; (5) relative success while neglecting easy pieces; and (6) relative success and without differentiating change.

Golembiewski's discussion of these ironies is essential for OD specialists. Managers and students of organizations who have a background in social science methods, statistics, and OD can understand the book. The following paragraphs cover each irony, and provide a constructive criticism.

(1) Golembiewski documents high success rates from OD interventions in public (84 percent), private (89 percent), and Third World (72 percent) organizations. These findings should quell pessimism about practice, though the success bias presented in published materials and from OD practitioners needs closer scrutiny.

(2) Golembiewski's learning models improve praxis. His degenerative and regenerative interaction models are value-laden and discussed throughout the book. Three models of discrepancies between the ideal and the actual organizational settings, and related change efforts, directly address this irony. The schema for configurational analysis presented in the last chapter receives scant attention and may provide the best learning model.

(3) Golembiewski addresses several ethical and methodological questions when differentiating people to improve success. His discussion of using performance appraisals and surveys provides a valuable operational guide. This guide is essential for the statistical differentiation among employees. However, qualitative differentiation deserves more attention.

(4) Golembiewski prescribes a simple theory; if we can specify the organizational (small group) settings, we can tailor design variants. Specificity is based on conditions of agreement or disagreement in small groups and the degree of psychological burnout experienced. Designs can vary based on diagnoses, but Golembiewski provides some cogent guidelines for design selection. Golembiewski's fine tuning the OD design to reduce employee burnout and turnover needs better testing for threats to internal validity.

(5) By using limited-purpose interventions (easy pieces), flexible work hours and a "demotion experience," Golembiewski maintains that one can "set the stage" for non-incremental cultural change in an organization. Golembiewski's discussion of these interventions is outstanding, and I have no criticism. The flextime intervention analysis is convincing as a means to increase productivity and the demotion experience will become an important tool in the OD practitioner's arsenal.

(6) Golembiewski maintains that change in organizations must be specified. He uses experimental designs with appropriate checks on validity to solidify his argument. His alpha, beta, and gamma change categories have conceptual appeal. His emphasis is on existential states and behavioral contours. He believes that estimates of change in organizations have been too conservative and the current technological advances (factor analysis) will allow the measuring of gamma or "big bang" change. The information presented in the figures and graphs could be improved in this chapter and throughout the book.

In the final analysis, every irony discussed improves OD success. Golembiewski has strengthened OD with his well-documented effort. The reader should be left with the impression that this book will have a major impact on OD theory and practice in the 1990s.

Subject Terms:

> Ironies in Organizational Development (Book)
> Organizational change

Hinrichs, G. (2004). Meaning from the media. *Organization Development Journal*, *22*(1), pp. 111-113.

Focuses on organization development (OD) practitioners' favorite media clips and meeting designs used to create experiential learning. Metaphor for a team bringing in transformational change to their organization; Advantages of experiential learning; Types of media used to share effective approaches to experiential learning

Subject Terms:

>Organizational behavior
>Corporate culture
>Organizational change
>Organizational structure
>Experiential learning
>Active learning

Hinrichs, G. (2009). Organic organizational design. *OD Practitioner, 41*(4), pp. 4-11.

The article offers information on the functions of an organic organizational design. Organizational design refers to the creative process of designing and aligning elements to efficiently and effectively deliver organizational purpose. It cites the elements must be considered in organizational design such as people, processes, and systems. It presents a case study on the design approaches of nonprofit organization Positive Change Core (PCC).

Subject Terms:

> Organizational structure
> Organizational effectiveness
> Core competencies
> Strategic planning
> Nonprofit organizations
> Case studies
> Complex systems

Hoberecht, S., Joseph, B., Spencer, J., & Southern, N. (2011, Fall). Inter-organizational network: An emerging paradigm of whole systems change. *OD Practioner, 43*(4), pp. 23-27.

The article discusses the significant role of Interorganizational Networks (ION) for organizations driving a sustainable development agenda. It explains that ION creates an environment for collaboration and to promote collaborative behaviors for a deep commitment to support sustainable communities locally and globally. It notes that virtual collaboration and organizational development (OD) professionals enable organizational collaboration to profitable yet sustainable business practices.

Subject Terms:

      Interorganizational networks
      Sustainable development
      Organizational change
      Social responsibility of business
      Community organization

Holt, D. T., Dorey, E. L., Bailey, L. C., & Low, B. R. (2009). Recovering when a change initiative stalls. *OD Practitioner*, *41*(1), pp. 20-24.

The article offers a look at the recovery following the suspension of change initiative. It states that once the change effort stalls, a different approach is necessary to create readiness and overcome resistance. The article is of the view that the methods that work when change is initiated for the first time might not work as part of the recovery. Therefore, to efficiently and effectively move organizations through these stages, leaders are encouraged to use facilitation strategies. There are problems as well which include constraints such as budget or time.

Subject Terms:

Organizational change
Change management
Problem solving
Budget
Organizational effectiveness
Industrial efficiency
Strategic planning
Preparedness

Hoover, J. D. (2008). Cognitive mapping and diagnostic aspects of organizational change. *Organization Development Journal*, *26*(1), pp. 37-44.

A model of Perceptual Actualization, as a whole person phenomenon based upon processes of experiential learning, is presented. The enactment of Perceptual

Actualization elements is demonstrated as essential to successful execution of the diagnostic aspects of organizational change. The model, utilizing aspects of cognitive mapping, serves as a framing template illuminating those diagnostic variables that are operative (actualized). The paper concludes with examples of pathways to successful change diagnosis and implementations.

Subject Terms:

> Organizational change
> Organizational behavior
> Personnel management
> Organizational structure
> Organizational effectiveness
> Organizational learning
> Experiential learning
> Active learning
> Learning by discovery

Howard, C., Logue, K., Quimby, M., & Schoeneberg, J. (2009). Framing change. *OD Practitioner, 41*(1), pp. 25-31.

The article offers a look at how organizations manage ongoing change and development. It refers to the book "Reframing Organizations," by L.G. Bolman and

T.E. Deal, in which they state that the ability to utilize multiple frameworks is a foil for blindness that paralyzes organizations. It looks at four different frameworks that create a broader system-level perspective. They are: structural which define organizational hierarchy and responsibility, human resources which define how organizations manage and motivate employees, political which relates to gain and loss of organizational power and symbolic which relates to organizational culture.

Subject Terms:

> Organizational change
> Personnel management
> Organizational behavior
> Corporate culture
> Employee motivation
> Responsibility

Huang, X., Kristal, M., & Schroeder, R. G. (2010). The impact of organizational structure on mass customization capability: A contingency view. *Production & Operations Management*, *19*(5), pp. 515-530.

This study investigates the role of organizational structure in facilitating the development of mass customization (MC) capability in various manufacturing settings. Specifically, three dimensions of organizational structure are considered-flatness, centralization, and employee multifunctionality. We model organizational structure as a second-order factor whose value is captured on a mechanistic-organic continuum, where the organic form is characterized by a flat, decentralized structure with a wide use of multifunctional employees. We propose that a positive relationship exists between the organic organizational structure and MC capability. Additionally, building upon contingency theory, we argue that this positive relationship is moderated by mass customizer type-full mass customizers, which customize products at the design or fabrication stage of the production cycle, versus partial customizers, which customize products only at the assembly or delivery stages. Based on a study of 167 manufacturing plants from three industries and eight countries, we find that, for the overall sample, organic structure plays a significant role in enabling firms to pursue MC capability. However, an analysis of full versus partial mass customizers shows that the positive impact of organic structure on MC capability is statistically significant only for full mass customizers, not for partial mass customizers.

Subject Terms:

> Mass customization
> Organizational structure
> Contingency theory (Management)
> Decentralization in management
> Employees
> Research
> Factories

Hultman, K. (2004). Let's wipe out systemic mistrust. *Organization Development Journal*, *22*(1), pp. 102-106.

The author offers advice to organization development (OD) practitioners on how to eliminate systemic mistrust in the system. The article also mentions the effects of systemic mistrust on corporate culture and definition of systemic mistrust.

Subject Terms:

Management
Organizational behavior
Corporate culture
Organizational change
Organizational sociology
Organizational structure

Hutton, C., & Liefooghe, A. (2011, March 01). Mind the gap: Revisioning organization development as pragmatic reconstruction. *Journal of Applied Behavioral Science, 47*(1), pp. 76-97.

This article identifies the possibilities for a revisioning of organization development (OD) in light of a resurgent debate within both OD and the wider field of organization studies. Scholar-practitioner, theory-practice, and relevance-rigor are terms within the debate that indicate what are seen as the challenges. In the context of this debate, the authors review the theory and practice of New OD and Critical Discourse Analysis (CDA) both as sources of insights into approaches to OD and organizational change and as pointers to the gaps along the way of seeking to address these challenges. The authors discuss what else can be learned from approaches that are based on concepts of organization practice. In light of this understanding, the authors argue for a revisioning of OD as a process of engaged inquiry that changes organizations by changing their practices.

Subject Terms:

> Organization development
> Discourse
> Practice
> Pragmatism

Hyde, C. (2004). Multicultural development in human services agencies: Challenges and solutions. *Social Work, 49*(1), pp. 7-16.

Comprehensive multicultural organizational development (MCOD) is increasingly necessary in human services agencies. This article presents results from an exploratory study that identified challenges and solutions to MCOD, against the backdrop of daily realities of agency life. The author conducted interviews with 20 consultants and 20 practitioners experienced in MCOD. Qualitative analysis revealed four challenges--socioeconomic environment, organizational dynamics, conceptualization of the change effort, and consultant competence; and four solutions--collaborative environmental relations, leadership development, assessment and planning, and consultant selection. Results suggest the complexities of MCOD and ways that human services agencies can sustain such efforts.

Subject Terms:

    Cultural Diversity
    Organizational Change
    Social Work

Ittner, C. D., & Larcker, D. F. (1997). Product development cycle time and organizational performance. *Journal of Marketing Research (JMR)*, *34*(1), pp. 13-23.

The authors develop and test a simple conceptual model linking product development cycle time to organizational performance. Using data from two industries (automobile arid computer) and four countries (Canada, Germany, Japan, and the United States), they find that faster cycle time alone is not associated with higher accounting returns, sales growth, or perceived overall performance. Stronger support is found for the hypothesis that some product development practices, such as cross-functional teams and advanced design tools, interact with accelerated product development to improve performance, whereas other practices, such as reverse engineering of competitors' products, suppress the potential benefits from lower cycle times. Finally, interaction effects for other organizational practices, such as customer involvement in the product development process and the extent to which new technology is obtained from external sources, appear to vary by industry.

Subject Terms:

    Product launches
    First-mover advantage
    Competitive advantage
    Market entry
    Manufacturing processes
    Product design
    Sales
    Commercial; products
    Marketing strategy
    Profit maximization
    Organizational effectiveness
    Success in business

Iverson, K., & Vukotich, G. (2009). OD 2.0: Shifting from disruptive to innovative technology. *OD Practitioner, 41*(2), pp. 43-49.

The article discusses the significance of Web 2.0 in the organization development (OD). It outlines the expanding use of Web 2.0 in businesses, and relates how technological advances have increased the sales and marketing arena, as well as the employee engagement in an organization. It highlights the advantages of Web 2.0 since it offers more personalized and interactive first generation web applications, and provides opportunities for OD practitioners to participate in proactive discussion, sharing, connectivity and collaboration. It points out the need for practitioners to feel comfortable with the new technologies as it increases organizational effectiveness

Subject Terms:

> Web services
> Internet
> Organizational change
> Organizational effectiveness
> Management -- Employee participation
> Organizational behavior
> High technology
> Management
> Leadership

Jackson, H. K. (2010). The life of a black change agent and OD consultant. *OD Practitioner*, *42*(2), pp. 10-13.

A personal narrative is presented which the author's experience on being a consultant of Organization Development (OD) to change hostility against the Black people in the U.S.

Subject Terms:

Organizational change

Jamieson, D. W., & Vogel, J. A. (2010). From the guest editors. *OD Practitioner*, *42*(4), pp. 1-2.

The article discusses various reports published within the issue, including one by Matt Minahan on the need to separate organization development (OD) from human resources (HR), one by Susan Sweem on the emergence of HR strategic business partner role, and one by Martin Goldberg and Claudy Jule on the differentiated lenses of OD and HR.

Subject Terms:

    Organizational change
    Personnel management

Jamieson, D. W., & Vogel, J. A. (2010). Upcoming special issues of the OD Practitioner. *OD Practitioner*, *42*(3), pp. 2-3.

The article presents the topics that will be discussed in the fall 2010 and winter 2011 issues of the journal as well as its review board members as of 2010. It highlights the scope of the topics in the coming issues including organizational effectiveness, human resource and organizational development (OD) functions, and OD approaches that meet organizational challenges. It also offers information on three review board members namely Cathy L. Royal, Anne Litwin, and Claire B. Halverson.

Subject Terms:

    Organizational effectiveness
    Organizational change
    Personnel management

Jaques, T. (2010). Reshaping crisis management: The challenge for organizational design. *Organization Development Journal, 28*(1), pp. 9-17.

A new approach to crisis management is emerging, which progresses beyond a purely reactive response and creates fresh opportunities for improved organizational development. This paper outlines the traditional event approach to crisis management, which focuses on preparing for and responding to a major adverse occurrence, and discusses the new process approach, which reshapes crisis management within a broader continuum of management activity. Crisis prevention instead of just crisis response necessitates moving responsibility from the operational to the executive level. The paper builds on a nonlinear model to explore how crisis management activities can be clustered together and integrated to optimize organizational effectiveness.

Subject Terms:

> Crises management
> Organizational change
> Organizational structure
> Problem solving
> Organizational effectiveness
> Industrial efficiency
> Organizational sociology
> Mathematical models
> Nonlinear models (Statistics)

Joanna, E., & Flejszman, A. (2010). New management system as an instrument of implementation sustainable developmental concept at organizational level. *Technological & Economic Development of Economy, 16*(2), pp. 202-218.

This article is discussing several different topics such as diversity of contemporary management concepts, short life duration of some of them, and fashion of implementing popular solutions. The author also mentions indiscriminate adoption of management systems in companies simultaneously with a long period of waiting for positive effects of implemented changes and decreasing involvement of employees lead to the situation in which many companies still face unresolved dilemma of choosing the right strategy of acting that ensures sustainable development of a unit. Therefore, new solutions should be treated as one of the elements of organization improvement, not as an objective as such, and as the way of solving the existing problems. One of the ways of realizing sustainable development principles at the level of an organizational unit is implementation of normalized systems elaborated by International Organization for Standardization (ISO). The article presents a proposal of the way of implementing sustainable development concept at organizational level using three systems: quality, environmental, occupational health and safety management.

Subject Terms:

> Industrial management
> Sustainable development
> Organizational change
> Industrial hygiene
> Management

Johnson, H. H. (2009). Implementing the triple bottom line-or not? *OD Practitioner, 41*(1), pp. 50-53.

The article focuses on the opinion of three organizational development (OD) experts, Terry Terranova, Kathy Woodrich, and Nancy Ashworth to OD consultant Ann Telland, in handling the situation, which requires implementing a vaguely understood organizational initiative. Terranova advises Ann to determine if there is a need to implement such change. Woodrich advises Ann to identify opportunities and objectives for the action planning process. Ashworth proposes a five-phase change process.

Subject Terms:

> Organizational change
> Organizational accountability
> Consultants
> Goal (Psychology)

Johnson, H. H. (2011). The sustainability initiative at Metro Charity Hospital. *OD Practitioner*, *43*(4), pp. 40-43.

The article focuses on the initiative of Metro Charity Hospital, located in a major metropolitan area, to achieve sustainability. It mentions that organization development (OD) consultant Jen Han helped Mina Panos, who was chosen to head up a sustainability initiative at Metro, to take recycling of medical devices as a sustainable initiative. OD experts Tony Colatoni, Sharon Fletcher, and Carol Silk have claimed that Han is pointing Manos in the right direction.

Subject Terms:

> Sustainable development
> Organizational change
> Green business
> Environmental aspects

Johnson, J, & Lopes, J. (2008). The intergenerational workforce, revisited. *Organization Development Journal, 26*(1), pp. 31-36.

Factors associated with generational differences are explored as they pertain to the workplace and organizational life. The authors conclude there are little differences between fundamental motivations and organizational behavior across the various age groupings commonly used in popular literature and media. Organization development consultants and human resource managers may want to reconsider assumptions about developing and managing the multi- generational workforce.

Subject Terms:

Labor supply
Organizational change
Organizational behavior
Corporate culture
Work environment
Personnel management
Organizational effectiveness
Industrial management
Life span, Productive

Johnson-Cramer, M. E., Cross, R. L., & Yan, A. (2003). Sources of fidelity in purposive organizational change: Lessons from a re-engineering case. *Journal of Management Studies, 40*(7), pp. 1837-1870.

The debate between adaptation and inertia hinges on whether theorists believe that organizations can effect purposive organizational change in which the realized structures match the planned structures. To date, research on organizational change has yielded few insights into the conditions under which such change occurs. This longitudinal case study of a re-engineering program at a medium-sized bank examined the conditions under which elements of the planned structure were faithfully implemented. Elaborating a model of change fidelity, this paper argues that the features of the design elements themselves, attributes of the change process, and general contextual factors affect the likelihood that planned changes will occur.

Subject Terms:

    Organizational change
    Organizational structure
    Reengineering (Management)
    Banking industry
    Management
    Change management
    Job enrichment
    Division of labor
    Organization
    Personnel management
    Industrial management
    Adaptability (Psychology)

Jones, R. A., Jimmieson, N. L., & Griffiths, A. G. (2005). The impact of organizational culture and reshaping capabilities on change implementation success: The mediating role of readiness for change. *Journal of Management Studies, 42*(2), pp. 361-386.

It was hypothesized that employees' perceptions of an organizational culture strong in human relations values and open systems values would be associated with heightened levels of readiness for change which, in turn, would be predictive of change implementation success. Similarly, it was predicted that reshaping capabilities would lead to change implementation success, via its effects on employees' perceptions of readiness for change. Using a temporal research design, these propositions were tested for 67 employees working in a state government department who were about to undergo the implementation of a new end-user computing system in their workplace. Change implementation success was operationalized as user satisfaction and system usage. There was evidence to suggest that employees who perceived strong human relations values in their division at Time 1 reported higher levels of readiness for change at pre-implementation which, in turn, predicted system usage at Time 2. In addition, readiness for change mediated the relationship between reshaping capabilities and system usage. Analyses also revealed that pre-implementation levels of readiness for change exerted a positive main effect on employees' satisfaction with the system's accuracy, user friendliness, and formatting functions at post-implementation. These findings are discussed in terms of their theoretical contribution to the readiness for change literature, and in relation to the practical importance of developing positive change attitudes among employees if change initiatives are to be successful.

Subject Terms:

> Organizational change
> Corporate culture
> Employees -- Attitudes
> Interpersonal relations
> Organizational sociology
> Research
> State governments -- Officials & employees
> Systems integration
> Change management
> Innovation adoption
> Technology attitudes
> Preparedness
> Methodology

Joseph, L. E. (2010). Desire held captive: A journey of discovery and self-expression. *OD Practitioner, 42*(2), pp. 63-68.

A personal narrative is presented which explore the author's experience of being able to hide intelligence and to understand the perception and thinking of organizational development (OD) to attain real change in multicultural environment.

Subject Terms:

Organizational change

Jules, C. (2009). Feedback as a unit of work: A data-driven approach to organizational coaching. *OD Practitioner*, *41*(3), pp. 8-12.

The article illustrates how practitioners who are interested in coaching leaders in meeting business challenges can benefit from using organization development. It includes a case study in illustrating how unit of work, a Gestalt organizational and system development (OSD) conceptual frame, was used to design organization coaching process. Moreover, a summary of lessons that was provided as well as personal experiences are also discussed and note that the organizational coaching process is neither intervention nor a stand-alone single event.

Subject Terms:

> Organization
> Management
> Communication in organizations
> Organizational change
> Associations, institutions, etc.
> Organizational sociology
> Organizational growth
> Case studies
> Industrial -- Social aspects
> Social aspects
> Executive coaching

Kahnweiler, W. M. (2006). The development of OD careers: A preliminary framework for enacting what we preach. *Organization Development Journal, 24*(1), pp. 10-21.

Much attention has been given over the past several decades to enhancing OD as a profession. This includes but is not limited to the creation and refinement of core competencies for effective OD practice, practitioner certification processes, and academic preparation program accreditation systems. However, little if any literature has been devoted to how OD careers develop and flourish. This article reports on a study designed to address this gap in OD professionalization efforts. Based on in-depth interviews with 25 successful practitioners, a preliminary career development framework for those in OD and related professions is presented. It is posited that such a framework can assist OD professionals in their ongoing career development as well as provide researchers with some guidelines for future studies in this arena.

Subject Terms:

> Organizational change
> Career development
> Organizational structure
> Personnel changes
> Professional
> Professional employees

Kahnweiler, W. M. (2008). Opportunities for O.D. to address work-life issues. *Organization Development Journal*, *26*(4), pp. 59-65.

For more than 30 years, researchers and practitioners have devoted considerable attention to work-life issues. Surprisingly, there is a paucity of literature on work-life targeted specifically to O.D. professionals. The purpose of this article is to inform the O.D. community about some aspects of the broad and varied area of work-life that seem highly relevant to O.D. Specific opportunities for O.D. practitioners and researchers are offered.

Subject Terms:

> Industrial research
> Work -- Sociological aspects
> Organizational change
> Change management
> Organizational behavior
> Professional employees
> Businesspeople
> Life span, Productive
> Literature

Kahnweiler, W. M. (2010). Organization development success and failure: A case analysis. *Organization Development Journal*, *28*(2), pp. 19-28.

Positive publication bias appears to be the norm in O.D. literature. Because of this and for other reasons, published reports of failed and less than completely successful O.D. interventions should be more commonplace. This article discusses what constitutes success and failure in O.D., describes the inherent challenges in determining O.D. success and failure, and presents a case study and analysis of a less that fully successful O.D. intervention in a Fortune 50 global multinational corporation.

Subject Terms:

Case studies
Organizational change
Qualitative research
International business enterprises
Clients
Equity
Prejudices
Intervention (Social services)
Meta-analysis

Kahnweiler, W. M. (2011). Non-profit organizations: A primer for OD researchers and practitioners. *Organization Development Journal, 29*(4), pp. 81-89.

While Organization Development (OD) occurs in all 3 sectors, scant attention has been paid to the particular considerations, nuances, challenges, and opportunities pertaining to OD in the nonprofit sector. This article attempts to address this need by first presenting an overview of the Third Sector, its sub-sectors, and current issues and trends facing it. Next, some key differences between non-profit organizations and those in the public and private sectors are offered, which will hopefully enlighten OD professionals with little or no exposure to and experience in non-profit organizations (NPOs). Finally, implications for OD researchers and practitioners will be discussed.

Subject Terms:

    Organizational change
    Nonprofit sector
    Nonprofit organizations
    Public sector
    Private sector
    Economic sectors

Karakas, F. (2009). New paradigms in organization development: Positivity, spirituality, and complexity. *Organization Development Journal, 27*(1), pp. 11-26.

Traditional Organization development models are giving way to new intervention methods and models in an age of uncertainty, complexity, globalization, and accelerating change. The purpose of this article is to suggest new roles for Organization development professionals in the 21st century. Drawing from appreciative inquiry, positive organizational scholarship, spirituality, and complexity, the paper discusses the emergence of seven new creative roles for Organization development professionals: Social artist, ethical pioneer, spiritual visionary, creative catalyst, cultural innovator, holistic thinker, and community builder. This paper invites Organization development professionals and consultants to consider new paradigms/perspectives and to adopt new roles in organizational interventions for wider impact and better performance.

Subject Terms:

Organizational change
Globalization
International relations
Organizational structure
Organizational sociology
Spirituality
Creative ability
Holistic education
Social ethics

Keeffe, M. J., & Darling, J. R. (2008). Transformational crisis management in organization development: The case of talent loss at Microsoft. *Organization Development Journal, 26*(4), pp. 43-58.

The article reports on the importance of leadership role in transformational crisis management in the personal and organizational development in the U.S. As stated, in times of crisis, the most important thing to do is to maintain an open channel of communication and involving appropriate individuals within the organization. In times of crisis in both domestic and international business, it is a great opportunity for the managerial leaders to offer the exact leadership skills needed and to enhance the operational success of their organizations. In addition, Microsoft Corp. must be able to employ in transformational crisis management in a very effective, meaningful and opportunistic manner.

Subject Terms:

 Leadership
 Crises management
 Problem solving
 Conflict management
 Organizational change
 Communication
 Business enterprises
 Microsoft Network (Online service)

Kerber, K., & Buono, A. F. (2005). Rethinking organizational change: Reframing the challenge of change management. *Organization Development Journal*, *23*(3), pp. 23-38.

The article examines three basic approaches to organizational change-directed change, planned change, and guided changing-and their appropriateness as a function of the relative business complexity and socio-technical uncertainty in the situation. Two moderating factors, the change capacity of the organization and the urgency of the situation, are also considered. The article concludes with a discussion of the implications for our thinking about organizational change and change management practices.

Subject Terms:

      Research
      Organizational change
      Organizational behavior
      Communication in organizations
      Corporate culture
      Action research
      Methodology
      Social science research

Kezar, A. (2001). Future research on organizational change. *ASHE-ERIC Higher Education Report*, *28*(4), pp. 125-132.

The author discusses the main research areas about organizational change that could help leaders, policy-makers and institutions to allow higher education to thrive over the 21st century. Adaptation in higher education; Forces that can shape higher education; Need for some institutions to focus on the external environment more than others; Impact on change of the increasing bureaucratization of universities.

Subject Terms:

  Education -- Research
  Educational change
  Organizational change

Kezar, A. (2001). Providing a common language for understanding organizational change. *ASHE-ERIC Higher Education Report, 28*(4), pp. 11.

Describes some of the common concepts related to organizational change in higher education. These are common language, which refers to the reasons and methods of change; differentiation of change from other similar phenomena; ways in which change is broader than the concepts of innovation, diffusion, institutionalization, reform and adaptation; and sources or forces affecting a change process.

Subject Terms:

Organizational change
Educational change

Kezar, A. (2001). Theories and models of organizational change. *ASHE-ERIC Higher Education Report*, *28*(4), pp. 25.

The author discusses the necessity of models of organizational change in higher education. The article contains discussions about main typologies of organizational change; assessment of change at a macro level; ways in which each model of change represents a different ideology with its own assumptions about the nature of human beings and social organizations; and importance of reviewing the multidisciplinary research on change.

Subject Terms:

Organizational change
Educational change

Khan, A. (2011). Dictating change, shouting success: Where is accountability? *Australasian Accounting Business & Finance Journal*, 5(4), pp. 85-99.

A great body of literature suggests that the poor were better off before the microfinance sector's paradigm shift of the mid-1990s. The sector's 'dependent' constituents' focus changed in an effort to cope with the changes dictated by its 'controlling' constituents. This paper's key finding is that the not-for-profit sector, where beneficiaries' interests are at stake, and the corporate sector, where owners and management are separate, should undergo an externally dictated change only after passing through a regulating agency's scrupulous check, lest the change harm the sector's beneficiaries. The paper attempts to create awareness among policy-makers of the need to be thoughtful of the ultimate beneficiaries in similar cases of externally dictated organizational change.

Subject Terms:

      Organizational change
      Social responsibility of business
      Microfinance
      Nonprofit organizations
      Industrial policy
      Financial services industry

Khatir, F. (2010). Never a prophet in your own country. *OD Practitioner*, *42*(2), pp. 49-53.

A personal narrative is presented which explore the author's experience of being an international organization development (OD) practitioner to achieve cultural change.

Subject Terms:

Organizational change

Kim, J. (2011). Abstract from the Academy of Management: Organizational structure and change processes in long-term care: A configurational approach. *Journal of Healthcare Management, 56*(6), pp. 419-420.

An abstract of the article "Organizational Structure and Change Processes in Long-Term Care: A Configurational Approach" by Jungyoon Kim is presented.

Subject Terms:

Organizational change
Organizational structure
Long-term care of the sick

Kimberly, J. R., & Bouchikhi, H. (1995). The dynamics of organizational development and change: How the past shapes the present and constrains the future. *Organization Science, 6*(1), pp. 9-18.

The article focuses on organizational theory and the challenges posed by changing organizational conditions and managerial demands. It examines the analytical importance of understanding how and why organizations grow and develop. It states researchers need a longitudinal perspective to understand the developmental dynamics of organizations. It mentions that the pluralistic nature of contemporary social inquiry has required researchers to utilize other methodologies and research methods, and suggests that biographical approaches are becoming increasingly legitimate.

Subject Terms:

Organizational change
Organizational behavior
Corporate culture
Organizational sociology
Organizational growth
Organizational research
Social sciences -- Biographical methods
Methodology
Comprehension
Longitudinal method

Kochikar, V. P., & Ravindra, M. P. (2007). Developing the capability to be agile. *Organization Development Journal, 25*(4), pp. 127-134.

Organizations must increasingly view their competency development challenges in terms of the need to be agile. This paper defines the notion of agile capability and deconstructs it into its constituent competencies. These competencies are depicted in the form of an agile capability 'stack' - a layered set of the competencies that collectively constitute agile capability. This deconstruction is carried out by instantiating the concept within one industry, the technology industry. However, the concept of agile capability is widely applicable. Our objective is to place the notion of agile capability firmly in organizational competency development discourse, and help its conscious cultivation.

Subject Terms:

> Organizational effectiveness
> Strategic planning
> Organizational change
> Management
> Personnel management
> Financial performance
> Business planning
> Change management
> Technology

Konczak, L. J. (2008). Organization change: Theory and practice. (2nd edition) by Burke W. Warner. *Personnel Psychology, 61*(4), pp. 942-946.

The article reviews the book "Organization Change: Theory and Practice" 2nd edition by Burke W. Warner: It's almost impossible to pick up a business periodical these days and not read about some type of changes occurring in businesses, both large and small. Recent articles in Fortune attest to the prevalence of change in today's organizations. Consider the cover-story articles that appeared earlier this year.

Subject Terms:

Organizational change
Book – Reviews

Kontoghiorghes, C., & Hansen, C. D. (2004). Identification of key predictors of rapid change adaptation. *Organization Development Journal, 22*(1), pp. 21-39.

The article reports on findings of a study of key predictors of change adaptation in a service organization. These are change adaptation in an organization setting within which there is an emphasis on process and quality improvement; organizational outcomes associated with rapid change; and contemporary significance of organizational change.

Subject Terms:

> Organizational change
> Organizational behavior
> Management
> Service industries
> Organizational sociology

Korten, F., Caluwe, L. d., & Geurts, J. (2010). The future of organization development: A Delphi study among Dutch experts. *Journal of Change Management* , *10*(4), pp. 393-405.

From this Delphi study among Dutch experts, the future of organization development (OD) emerges as a loosely coupled community of practice, linking very diverse members, professionals as well as scholars. One finds different priorities and values in this community, some of them even dilemmatic. The authors argue that diversity and complexity are strengths not weaknesses of a 'sustainable' OD. Referring to organizational concepts such as requisite variety and resilience, the authors stress that OD networks should, in the future more than in the past, make sure that a diverse set of ambitions can be discussed, promoted, fostered, accommodated and realized.

Subject Terms:

    Organizational change
    Delphi method
    Research

Kossek, E., Young, W., Gash, D. C., & Nichol, V. (1994). Waiting for innovation in the human resources department: Godot implements a human resource information system. *Human Resource Management*, *33*(1), pp. 135-159.

The implementation of a new human resource information system (HRIS) represents a major form of planned organizational change for the Human Resource function, yet little research has been conducted on this issue. This article presents a longitudinal case study of the reactions of the Human Resource community in a large energy company to the planned implementation of a new corporate HRIS. Implementing an HRIS to enhance strategic and business decision-making has important organizational development implications. A new HRIS (1) represents an attempt to enable Human Resources to become more of a business partner, (2) changes the nature of HR work to encompass a greater information broker and decision support role, and (3) alters power dynamics and communication patterns involving Human Resources. Varying levels of resistance and ambivalence were found regarding the extent to which human resource information systems skills were valued as a critical competency. While there is a trend, toward attitudinal convergence within the human resource community, over time, the results suggest that user skill level maybe more strongly related to variance in attitudes toward the value of a new HRIS than to hierarchical level or business unit affiliation. The study also found that face-to-face seminars were a significantly more effective intervention than was written communication in influencing favorable intention to use the HRIS.

Subject Terms:

    Personnel management
    Strategic planning -- Employee participation
    Business planning
    Decisions making
    Organizational change
    Management
    Organizational structure
    Problem solving
    Red tape
    Informational resources management
    Organizational behavior
    Study & teaching

Kraimer, M. L., Seibert, S. E., Wayne, S. J., Liden, R. C., & Bravo, J. (2011, May). Adcetedents and outcomes of organziational support for development: The critical role of career opportunities. *Journal of Applied Psychology, 96*(1), pp. 485-500.

This study examines antecedents and behavioral outcomes of employees' perceptions of organizational support for development. We first propose that employees' past participation in formal developmental activities and experience with developmental relationships positively relate to their perceptions of organizational support for development. We then propose that perceived career opportunity within the organization moderates the relationship between organizational support for development and employee performance and turnover. Using a sample of 264 exempt-level employees and their supervisors, we found that participation in training classes, leader-member exchange, and career mentoring were each positively related to employees' perceptions of organizational support for development. We also found support for the moderator hypotheses. Specifically, development support positively related to job performance, but only when perceived career opportunity within the organization was high. Further, development support was associated with reduced voluntary turnover when perceived career opportunity was high, but it was associated with increased turnover when perceived career opportunity was low. Our study demonstrates that social exchange and career motivation theory work together to explain when and how employees' perceptions of organizational support for development relate to turnover and job performance.

Krug, R. M. (2008). Fulfilling the promise of personal engagement: Recognizing realistic process requirements. *Organization Development Journal, 26*(1), pp. 63-68.

Engagement continues to play an important role in many organizations. The construct has been associated with various organizational benefits and, as such, has the potential for being an organization development (O.D.) tool. Contrary to the portrayal of engagement in several studies, this article contends that there is a cooperative relationship between the climatic conditions for engagement and organization-provided tactical tools. The establishment of this relationship will 1) enhance goal achievement and 2) provide support for a continued state of engagement.

Subject Terms:

Organizational change
Industrial organization
Personnel management
Organizational behavior
Organizational effectiveness
Communication in organizations
Teams in the workplace
Corporate culture
Engagement (Philosophy)

Kruglanski, A. W., Pierro, A., Higgins, E., & Capozza, D. (2007). "On the move" or "Staying put": Locomotion, need for closure, and reactions to organizational change. *Journal of Applied Social Psychology, 37*(6), pp. 1305-1340.

Four studies conducted in various organizations in Italy, employing contemporaneous and longitudinal designs, tested hypotheses relating 2 personality constructs—need for cognitive closure (Kruglanski & Webster, 1996) and locomotion tendency (Higgins, Kruglanski, & Pierro, 2003 ; Kruglanski et al., 2000)—to individuals' ability to successfully cope with organizational change. Across diverse organizational settings, populations studied, types of organizational change implemented, and measures of coping with change, we found that need for closure was negatively related, and locomotion tendency was positively related, to coping with change. We also found that the negative relation between need for closure and coping was attenuated where organizational climate is supportive of change, and that degree of successful coping with change determines post-change work attitudes.

Subject Terms:

      Organizational change
      Work attitudes
      Adaptability (Psychology)
      Organizational behavior
      Downsizing of organizations
      Adjustment (Psychology)
      Corporate turnarounds
      Personnel changes

Kruppa, R., & Meda, A. (2005). Group dynamics in the formation of a Ph.D. Cohort: A reflection in experiencing while learning organizational development theory. *Organization Development Journal, 23*(1), pp. 56-67.

This article is a reflection of two members of a PhD cohort's group dynamics as it came together to learn and experience Organizational Development (OD) theory in action. Much of the reflection was because of the Group Dynamics course experienced early in the PhD journey. The cohort consisted of twenty members who discovered and lived the theories of Block, Wheatley, Gersick, Tuckman, Homans, Goffman, Schein, Srivastva, Barrett, and others.

Subject Terms:

> Organizational change
> Management
> Corporate culture
> Industrial management
> Organizational behavior
> Social groups

Kruse, A. (2010). The ROI trap. *OD Practitioner*, *42*(3), pp. 48-52.

The article focuses on return on investment (ROI) in terms of initiatives and programs of organization development. It explains how the concept of ROI is implied and integrated to organization initiatives and programs with due respect to benefits or value side and investment or cost side. It offers suggestions on how to assess the value of business programs.

Subject Terms:

Rate of return
Organizational change
Organizational effectiveness
Business development
Business planning

Kuhn, M. H., & Griffith, D. B. (2010). Process solutions for HR/OD integration. *OD Practitioner*, *42*(4), pp. 52-57.

The article presents information on the works of the Indiana University-Purdue University, Indianapolis (IUPUI), and a public university focusing on research, which utilizes the integration of OD and HR in rendering consulting services. It features the training and organization development function of IUPUI's Human Resources Administration (HRA). The positive changes brought about by the development of OD function within HR, as well as the goals and moves of HRA to maximize such program are cited.

Subject Terms:

  Management
  Strategic planning
  Innovation adoption
  Consulting firms
  Public institutions

Kulick, O. A. (2006). Professionalism and OD: The past, the present and future scenarios. *Organization Development Journal*, *24*(3), pp. 20-32.

This article reviews the history of how occupations become professions. It also reports on the shifting power and alliances between capitalism, government, the professions and consumers. Organization development practitioners are encouraged to consider these concepts in their desire to achieve global professional status for O.D., especially with regard to the professional requirement for altruistic motivation and action.

Subject Terms:

    Organizational change
    Organizational behavior
    Professional orientations
    Occupations
    Professionalism
    Altruism

Kupiek, M. (2011). Neuro change: Enhancing traditional change management approaches through neuroscientific based concepts. *Neuropsychoeconomics Conference Proceedings*, pp. 37.

It is indicated that the success rate of change management projects varies between 30 to 40%. Even though any change project requires substantial investments in terms of money, time, and effort many undertakings fail. This paper investigates the potential contributions of current neuroscientific research results aimed at increasing the success rate of change management projects. An underlying change management framework based on systems theory and cognitive social psychology serves as reference for discussing selected findings of pertinent neuroscience research findings that will be presented and examined. The results indicate that there are some promising innovative approaches. A different perspective on a micro level, i.e. the individual and the team as well on the macro level, i.e. the organization provides first insight into how organizational change can be improved. I will show based on a neuroscientific concept of human personality that expectations, attention, and trust play a central role in changing organizations.

Subject Terms:

    Change management
    Organizational change
    Organizational structure
    Neuroscientific
    Cognitive psychology
    Social psychology

KyeHyeon, C., Gill, S. B., Gitonga, K. W., Seung Won, H., Macias, R., Meyer, J. P., & Ellinger, A. D. (2010). Human resource development, organization development, organizational learning, and organizational effectiveness: All needed more than ever. *Human Resource Development International, 13*(4), pp. 487-496.

The article presents an interview with Tim L. Reynolds, vice president of talent and organizational effectiveness for Whirlpool Corp. He beings by offering an overview of Whirlpool and how his global product organization is positioned within the company. He says that they deploy both human resource development (HRD) and organization development (OD) tactics corporately and at an organizational level. He further comments on the most important HRD/OD skill sets and competencies.

Subject Terms:

    Personnel management
    Organizational change
    Organizational effectiveness

Lacey, M. Y., Tompkins, T. C., & Egan, T. D. (2007). Curriculum implications based on analysis of internal consulting best practices. *Organization Development Journal, 25*(4), pp. 199-212.

The article presents the author's comments on the design of an organizational development (OD) curriculum. It reports that versatile intervention design should constitute OD for effective implementation of business strategy. It reflects that cross-cultural skills should be included in OD curriculum to allow internal OD practitioner to implement business strategies globally. It is noted that the curriculum should be flexible to accommodate latest OD innovations.

Subject Terms:

    Organizational change
    Business planning
    Innovations in business
    Strategic planning
    Editorials
    Study & teaching

Lalonde, C. (2007). Crisis management and organizational development: Towards the conception of a learning model in crisis management. *Organization Development Journal*, 25(1), pp. 17-26.

The field of crisis management currently faces two important limitations. First, this field has been distinguished by two major approaches to date, crisis management planning and analysis of organizational contingencies. However, despite what we have learned from these approaches, neither seems to lead to a crisis management learning model that fosters organizational resilience in coping with crises. Secondly, researchers have studied a number of events as case studies but have never synthesized these case studies. Consequently, each crisis seems idiosyncratic and administrators continue to repeat the same errors when a crisis occurs. The research proposal presented in this article1 aims to remove these limitations by bringing together two apparently opposing fields of study, that of crisis management, characterized by what are perceived as specific events, and that of organizational development, characterized by the strengthening of organizations capacities to cope with lasting changes. The author proposes to explore their potential to work together theoretically and empirically through a research design.

Subject Terms:

    Organization
    Management
    Organizational change
    Crisis management
    Empirical research
    Conflict management

Lamm, E., Gordon, J. R., & Purser, R. E. (2010). The role of value congruence in organizational change. *Organization Development Journal*, *28*(2), pp. 49-64.

This study investigates the relationship between perceived value congruence and behavioral support for organizational change. Value congruence is defined as the similarity between a person's values and those of the organization, similar to the notion of person-culture fit. The role of value congruence and its importance to organizational change is discussed. Survey results from 211 working MBA students and 95 employees in a non-profit agency indicate that value congruence is associated with behavioral support for organizational change. However, results found that some but not all types of value congruence were significant. Implications for theory and practice, and directions for future research are also presented.

Subject Terms:

      Organizational change
      Employees
      Organizational goals
      Survey
      Uncertainty
      Adaptability (Psychology)
      Perception
      Values
      Passivity (Psychology)

Landsbergis, P. A., & Vivona-Vaughan, E. (1995). Evaluation of an occupational stress intervention in a public agency. *Journal of Organizational Behavior, 16*(1), pp. 29-48.

Only in several controlled studies have organizational or situational stressors (in contrast to individuals) been targeted for change in order to reduce occupational stress. This study evaluates the impact of an intervention, which was based on organizational development, action research and Karasek's job strain model. Employee committees conducted problem diagnosis, action planning, and action taking in two departments in a public agency. Waiting list control departments and pre- post- and follow-up assessment were utilized. Results indicated a mixed impact of the intervention in one department, but a negligible or negative impact in the other. Obstacles to the effective implementation of the intervention strategy are discussed. These included a limited focus for the committees (department-wide rather than agency-wide), the negative impact of a major agency reorganization, and the lack of a more formal management and labor commitment to maintaining the stress reduction and organizational change process.

Subject Terms:

    Job stress
    Public companies
    Organizational change
    Work design
    Strategic planning -- Employee participation
    Collective bargaining
    Stress management
    Adaptability (Psychology)
    Social science research

Laszlo, A., & Laszlo, K. C. (2011). Systemic sustainability in OD practice: Bottom line and top line reasoning. *OD Practioner, 43*(4), pp. 10-16.

The article discusses the developmental process of greater systemic sustainability in organizational development (OD) practice. It explores the notions of top, triple and quadruple bottom lines reasoning which involves an economic, environmental, social, cultural component that needs to be developed in a soloed and non-integrated way for sustainability. Also cited are the ten dimensions of capital where organization can generate value including natural, financial, and social capital.

Subject Terms:

> Sustainable development
> Social responsibility of business
> Corporate environmentalism
> Infrastructure (Economics)
> Organizational change
> Corporate culture

Laszlo, A., Laszlo, K., & Johnsen, C. S. (2009). From high-performance teams to evolutionary learning communities: New pathways in organizational development. *Journal of Organizational Transformation & Social Change, 6*(1), pp. 29-48.

Developments in organizational thinking often lead to new forms of organizational structure. Increases in organizational complexity and operational connectivity have intensified the need for coordinated decision taking at and among all levels of organization. This means that the ability to work in teams has become a core competence in work environments where collaboration is at a premium. Empowered teams consist of people with complementary skills who are committed to a common purpose or a set of performance goals for which they hold themselves mutually accountable. The power and authority traditionally held exclusively by the manager is passed to the team. Contemporary organizations often demonstrate examples of such work teams, showing exceptional job performance and production of innovative solutions. Consequently, there has been great interest in understanding what makes these teams what they are, and how they function. This article reports on the characteristics of high-performance teams found in the study of a particular case and explores the possibilities – and implications – for developing high-performance teams into evolutionary learning communities. The significance of this research resides in the focus it lends to advancing beyond the traditional operational benchmark of the high-performance team to a new benchmark identified as the evolutionary learning community. Organizations that embrace this new construct not only raise the bar in terms of team standards for efficient, effective and efficacious operations but also create organizational dynamics that foster quality of work life and business cultures that are vibrant, alive and thriving.

Subject Terms:

> Organizational structure
> Organization
> Work environment
> Job performance
> Executives
> Learning

Lega, F., & Calciolari, S. (2012). Coevolution of patients and hospitals: How changing epidemiology and technological advances create challenges and drive organizational innovation. *Journal of Healthcare Management*, *57*(1), pp. 17-33.

Over the last 20 years, hospitals have revised their organizational structures in response to new environmental pressures. Today, demographic and epidemiologic trends and recent technological advances call for new strategies to cope with ultra-elderly frail patients characterized by chronic conditions, high-severity health problems, and complex social situations. The main areas of change surround new ways of managing emerging clusters of patients whose needs are not efficiently or effectively met within traditional hospital organizations. Following the practitioner and academic literature, we first identify the most relevant clusters of new kinds of patients who represent an increasingly larger share of the hospital population in developed countries. Second, we propose a framework that synthesizes the major organizational innovations adopted by successful organizations around the world. We conclude by substantiating the trends of and the reasoning behind the prospective pattern of hospital organizational development.

Subject Terms:

    Organizational change
    Change management
    Hospital wards
    Patient-centered care

Levin, I., & Gottlieb, J. Z. (2009). Realigning organization culture for optimal performance: Six principles & eight practices. *Organization Development Journal, 27*(4), pp. 31-46.

Organization culture can be a strong enabler or an insurmountable obstacle to implementing change in organizations. Most organization change efforts require some degree of culture shift. Yet changing an organization's culture continues to be a highly challenging and often elusive endeavor. After all, culture by definition provides stability, continuity, and predictability to organizational life. This article discusses six principles and eight practices for realigning organization culture to support and facilitate the achievement of strategic change goals. The principles address common errors made and the practices offer an integrated, comprehensive roadmap for culture change. The principles and practices are discussed in the context of the relevant literature and several examples from the consulting work of the authors are provided to illustrate application and approaches.

Subject Terms:

>Corporate culture
>Organizational change
>Change management
>Strategic planning
>Organizational effectiveness
>Business development
>Organizational goals
>Organizational behavior
>Corporation
>Sociology aspects

Lindy, C., & Reiter, P. (2006). The financial impact of staff development. *The Journal of Continuing Education in Nursing, 37*(3), pp. 121-127.

According to the 2002 annual report of the American Society for Training and Development (Van Buren & Erskine, 2002), the total training expenditure per employee in health care was $284, compared with an expenditure of $408 in 1999. According to Fischer (1999), staff development educators reported a lack of support and financial resources for education. [...] budgeting provides a framework to evaluate the organization's bottom line.

Subject Terms:

    Budgets
    Training
    Nurses
    Guidelines

Lips-Wiersma, M., & Hall, D. T. (2007). Organizational career development is not dead: A case study on managing the new career during organizational change. *Journal of Organizational Behavior, 28*(6), pp. 771-792.

New forms of careers have received increased attention in contemporary organizational research. A prominent focus in this research has been whether and how, in an increasingly unpredictable career environment, individuals are taking responsibility for their own career development. The implication is that career is becoming less central to organizational management practices. At the same time there is evidence that organizational changes typically described in this literature (such as delayering the organization in a quest for flexibility) have had a negative impact on career progress, resulting in resistance to change. The implication here is that career concerns are more central to organizational management practices. This in-depth qualitative case study examines whether individuals do in fact take more responsibility for their career development during times of organizational change. We also examine whether this does indeed mean that the organization takes less responsibility for career management. Our data indicate that individuals are, in fact, taking more responsibility for their own careers. At the same time we found that the organization in our case study also became more actively involved in career development and management. However, this active approach did not resemble traditional top-down career management and development. To us, the pattern of organizational and individual career development actions appear to constitute a kind of 'organizational dance,' a highly interactive mutual influence process, in which both parties are at once the agent and the target of career influence. Strengths and limitations of the study are discussed, as are directions for future research.

Subject Terms:

> Career development
> Organizational change
> Career changes
> Management
> Executive ability (Management)
> Research
> Case studies
> Adaptability (Psychology)
> Resistance to change

Liu, S. (2009). Organizational culture and new service development performance: Insights of knowledge intensive business service. *International Journal of Innovation Management, 13*(3), pp. 371-392.

Current research on new service development (NSD) management has resulted in an impressive amount of literature on the success factors of new service development, but there is little literature on NSD organizational culture. The purpose of this study was to assess the relationship between organization culture and NSD performance. Data were collected via questionnaires through face-to-face interviews with KIBS managers knowledgeable about NSD in their organization (sample size 192). The set correlation analysis was chosen to assess and evaluate the relationship between organization culture and NSD performance. Research results indicate that there exist strongly complementary relationships among innovative supportive culture, market orientation culture, learning culture and customer communication culture. This study outlines that the NSD management should perform to foster the different NSD organizational culture together and thereby enhance the performance of new service development activities.

Subject Terms:

Corporate culture
Organizational behavior
Corporations
Product orientation
Marketing strategy
Sociological aspects

Lopes da Costa, R., & Santos António, N. (2011). The "Outsourcing" as an instrument of competitiveness in the business consulting industry. *Journal of Management Research*, *3*(1), pp. 1-13.

In an era of particularly intense competition, the consulting services are becoming an increasingly important source of aid for strategy making and an important way to increase efficiency and quality in the various business activities. Many managers consider the consulting services as an influential and powerful tool for organizational change, bringing new life to the organization. The purpose of this article is to study this situation. We will carry out a study in one of the biggest Portuguese private bank, in order to show the real value of management consultancy. This study combines a broad view of business to study a set of skills. These skills are closely linked to the relationship between service and market and, when it is focusing on "core" competencies, resources and offers increasingly facilitating the wellbeing of the client, i.e. showing how a company can foster creativity and dynamism in the activities of companies when operates through the potentials of TIG (information technology management).

Subject Terms:

> Contracting out
> Organizational change
> Organizational effectiveness
> Information technology
> Management
> Industrial efficiency
> Business consultants

Lövey, I., & Avar, T. (2010). Co-creating a new world of organizations and communities - dialogue and action. *OD Practitioner*, *42*(1), pp. 44-47.

In August 2010, Hungary will host the Organizational Development World Summit (ODWS), an event that will be the first ever to assemble many of the global OD professional organizations. The main organizer of the conference, the Hungarian Association of Organization Developers (Szervezetfejlesztok Magyarországi Társasága (SZMT)), expects around 500-700 participants in Budapest, primarily OD professionals, CEOs, HR leaders, organization professionals, researchers, and leaders of non-conventional organizations from around the world. The initiative provides a unique opportunity for those involved in the world of OD to create new professional relations and collaborations while refreshing and reinforcing old ones. It is an event not to be missed not only by those belonging to the profession, but also managers, CEOs, and HR professionals.

Subject Terms:

    Conferences & conventions
    Organizational Development

Lumpkin, G. T., & Dess, G. G. (1995). Simplicity as a strategy making process: The effects of stage of organizational development and environment on performance. *Academy of Management Journal, 38*(5), pp. 1386-1407.

This field study investigated the importance of simplicity as a strategy-making process. Consistent with our hypotheses, use of a simplistic strategy-making process was found to be positively associated with performance during early stages of organizational development but detrimental to performance as organizations grew and matured. Simplicity was also found to be negatively related to performance in dynamic environments; in heterogeneous environments, it seemed to be adversely related to performance only in later stages of organizational development.

Subject Terms:

    Strategic planning
    Organizational change
    Industrial management
    Business planning
    Organizational effectiveness
    Success in business
    Corporations – Growth
    Organizational goals
    Performance – Management
    Decisions making
    Industrial efficiency
    Simplicity

Maes, J. D., Mosely Sr., D. C., & Mosley Jr., D. C. (2009, Spring). The sustainability of an O.D. intervention: A professional firm's movement toward empowerment and teamwork. *Organization Development Journal, 27*(1), pp. 79-91.

The article focuses on the sustainability of an organizational development (O.D.) intervention through a firm's movement toward empowerment and teamwork in the U.S. It highlights the professional journey of professional organization and an architectural firm Tsoi/Kobus & Associates (TK&A) toward empowerment and its shift toward a participative management system. It notes that TK&A was founded in 1983 by Edward Tsoi and Richard Kobus during the time when the O.D. intervention was first employed. It concludes that when times are difficult, organizations are forced to search for ways to survive and when things are going well, it takes visionary leadership and commitment to move ahead.

Subject Terms:

> Organizational change
> Sustainable development
> Employee empowerment
> Teams in the workplace
> Professional associations
> Development leadership

Maitland, E., & Sammartino, A. (2012). Flexible footprints: Reconfiguring MNCs for new value opportunities. *California Management Review*, *54*(2), pp. 92-117.

Powerful technological, regulatory, and economic forces compel the senior executives of multinational corporations (MNCs) to repeatedly re-evaluate and reconfigure value chains in the search for ongoing competitive advantage. However, releasing assets from existing activities and redeploying them to new opportunities is a challenging and poorly understood task. In particular, the standard strategic management concepts of use- and firm- flexibility overlook the crucial international dimension of location. Utilizing examples from GM, Qantas, and a mining MNC, this article argues that strategic flexibility should be consciously measured along all three dimensions. By using, the decision tool set out in this article, MNC executives can map their worldwide footprint of strategic roadblocks and opportunities to expand into new markets, divest redundant businesses, and build flexibility to adapt to future challenges.

Subject Terms:

International business enterprises
Value chains
Competitive advantage
Strategic planning
Theory of the firm
Decisions making
Organizational change
Expansion (Business)
Business planning
Decision trees

Mandysova, I. (2011). Regional development as result of company management strategic choice. *Economics & Management, 16,* pp. 567-570.

In the contemporary regional science, we criticize the lack of insufficiency and secondary role that is given to the micro-level, and to the importance of the personality of the entrepreneur and his business. The paper analyzes theories of regional development vis-à-vis organization theories. Regional development theories derive its behavior and operation of the business largely by the environment in which it is located. Our study stresses second aspect, which methodologically proceeds in the opposite direction. The environment the company operates in can be considered because of corporate behavior and its activities. This perspective offers much greater freedom of choice for organizations. It dedicates great attention to the decisions made by management and to the organizational structures deep within the enterprise.

Subject Terms:

    Community development
    Entrepreneurship
    Industrial management
    Organizational behavior
    Organizational structure

Marks, M., Warrick, D. D., & Meeks, M. (2011). Should OD be taught to undergraduates? Recommendations for business schools. *Organization Development Journal*, *29*(1), pp. 97-106.

A strong case can be made that Organization Development (OD) is a rapidly growing field that provides essential knowledge and skills that undergraduates need if they are going to be successful in times of dynamic change. However, if OD courses are available at all, most business schools offer them at the masters and doctorate levels only. In this study, we investigate prevailing views regarding whether OD should be taught to undergraduates and make recommendations for business schools based on the findings.

Subject Terms:

    Organizational change
    Business schools
    Job skills
    Study & teaching
    Curricula
    Undergraduate

Marshak, R. J. (2004). Morphing: The leading edge of organizational change in the 21st Century. *Organization Development Journal*, *22*(3), pp. 8-21.

Incremental and 'start-stop' models and methods of change developed during the Industrial Age are insufficient to address the needs of contemporary organizations operating in hyperactive environments. The concept of continuous whole-system change or 'morphing' is introduced along with the basic ideas, principles and requirements for how to engage in it. Implications for organization development, including needs for new theories and practices of organizational consulting and change are identified and discussed.

Subject Terms:

    Organizational change
    Organization
    Industrial organization
    Industrial management
    Management

Marshak, R. J. (2012). The Tao of change Redux. *OD Practitioner*, *44*(1), pp. 44-51.

The article explores the East-West assumptions concerning organizational change following the speculation about culturally based differences in East-West learning styles. It mentions some potential implications for the theory and practice of organization development (OD). It also reveals that the primary model of change involved in most OD theory and practice is the three-stage change processes of unfreezing, movement, and refreezing formulated by Kurt Lewin.

Subject Terms:

    Organizational change
    Cross-cultural differences
    Theory
    Cognitive styles

Marshak, R. J., & Bushe, G. R. (2009, Sep.). Further reflections on diagnostic and dialogic forms of organziation development. *Journal of Applied Behavioral Science, 45*(3), pp. 378-383.

In this article, the authors discuss the diagnostic and dialogic forms of organization development (OD). The authors explore the academic and practitioner communities regarding the premises and practices associated with OD. The authors argue the possible forms of OD in terms of theoretical and philosophical premises.

Marshak, R. J., & Grant, D. (2008). Transforming talk: The interplay of discourse, power, and change. *Organization Development Journal, 26*(3), pp. 33-40.

This article presents ideas about language, power, and organizational change from the new academic field of Organizational Discourse. These ideas expand our understanding of the importance of conversation, context, and contention as critical variables in socially constructing change. Three key ideas include: 1) change is created by changing the discourse(s), 2) new shared realities are created by fostering social agreement on new discourses, and 3) power processes are central to the creation and change of discourses.

Subject Terms:

    Organizational change
    Communication in organizations
    Business models
    Strategic planning
    Organizational effectiveness
    Social interaction
    Language & languages
    Social constructionism
    Philosophy

Marshak, R. J., & Grant, D. (2011, Summer). Creating change by changing the conversation. *OD Practioner, 43*(3), pp. 2-7.

The article focuses on the summary of a range of theory and research on language and change, wherein discourse is utilized to include conversations, written texts, and stories in organizational development (OD). It states that discourse plays a vital role in the creation of social reality because it establishes, reinforces, and challenges prevailing premises. It adds that change agents should influence the levels of discourse including intrapersonal, interpersonal and group, and socio cultural.

Marshall, T., & Lancaster, C. M. (2005). Comparing appreciative inquiry to action research: OD Practitioner perspectives. *Organization Development Journal, 23*(2), pp. 29-49.

This study examines the assumptions, approaches, and implications of appreciative inquiry (AI) and action research (AR) for organization development (OD) from the perspective of OD practitioners who use AI as an intervention approach. Interviews were conducted with OD practitioner informants to explore the strengths and weaknesses of AI compared to those of AR. Practitioners outlined the strengths and weaknesses of AI and AR and elaborated on ways that AI complements AR and other intervention approaches.

Subject Terms:

    Research
    Organizational change
    Organizational behavior
    Communication in organizations
    Corporate culture
    Action research
    Methodology
    Social science research

Martin, A. J., Jones, E. S., & Callan, V. J. (2005). The role of psychology cliamte in facilitating employee adjustment during organizational change. *Europen Journal of Work and Organizational Psychology, 14*(3), pp. 263-289.

The current research tested a theoretical model of employee adjustment during organizational change based on Lazarus and Folkman's (1984) cognitive phenomenological framework. The model hypothesized that psychological climate variables would act as coping resources and predict improved adjustment during change.

Mastrangelo, P. M. (2009). Will employee engagement be hijacked or reengineered? *OD Practitioner*, *41*(2), pp. 13-18.

The article discusses the concept of employee engagement in an organization. It stresses the need for the leaders to secure and reengineer the employee engagement process in order to have safer and strategic behaviors in an organization. It notes on the best time and place in reengineering the engagement project from the introduction of the term and the education of the clients about the organization's goals. It outlines the opportunity for organization development (OD) specialist to use their skill and ability in addressing both employee engagement and business problems. It emphasizes the importance of conducting engagement survey among employees to know their thoughts and ideas.

Subject Terms:

Employee empowerment
Reengineering (Management)
Management -- Employee participation
Strategic planning -- Employee participation
Organizational structure
Organizational change
Organizational behavior
Employees
Survey

McCroskey, J. C., Richmond, V. P., Johnson, A. D., & Smith, H. T. (2004). Organizational orientations theory and measurement: Development of measures and preliminary investigations. *Communication Quarterly, 52*(1), pp. 1-14.

Four studies are reported which focus on organizational orientations theory and relevant measuring instruments. An initial study designed to develop measures of the three components believed to constitute organizational orientations (upward mobile, indifferent, and ambivalent) is reported. Since it was believed that valid measures of organizational orientations should be associated with the way workers communicate, a second study designed to determine the association of organizational orientations with communication apprehension, immediacy, assertiveness, responsiveness, and job satisfaction was conducted as a preliminary validity test. Results of the first two studies pointed to both the reliability and the validity of the new measures. A third study was conducted which included new items designed to increase the reliability of the scales. The results generated revised measures with higher reliability. The fourth study was designed to expand the validation of the instruments by testing their associations with temperament, job satisfaction, and subordinates' perceptions of the credibility of their supervisors. Results suggest that the organizational orientations are associated with the "BIG THREE" temperament variables (extraversion, neuroticism, psychoticism) and are predictive of both job satisfaction and perceptions of supervisor credibility. Suggestions for future research and the limitations of the research program at this point are discussed.

Subject Terms:

    Communication
    Job satisfaction
    Organizational behavior
    Organization theory

McDonagh, J., & Coghlan, D. (2006). Information technology and the lure of integrating change: A neglected role for organizational development? *Public Administration Quarterly, 30*(1/2), pp. 22-55.

The article discusses information technology (IT) and integrated change for organizational development. The role of occupational groups in its perpetuation through time and a potential role for organization development are also discussed. An integrated approach to the introduction of IT accounts for economic, technical, human, and organizational facets of change. Introduction of IT into work organizations offers a potent arena in which organizational actors are regularly drawn into a milieu of intense discord. Promoting coordination and integration through effective use of information technology is increasingly a strategic priority for executive management.

Subject Terms:

Information technology
Organizational change
Occupational
Occupational structure
Industrial design coordination
Executives
Organizational behavior
Office management
Workforce planning
Sociological aspects

McFillen, J. M. (2006). Building O.D.C. as an academic discipline: A change leadership perspective. *Organization Development Journal, 24*(3), pp. 112-113.

The article discusses the establishment of organizational development and change as an academic discipline in a change leadership standpoint. The author relates a testimony that there is not only to the omnipresence and acceleration of change but also to the less hierarchical character of today's organizations.

Subject Terms:

    Universities & colleges
    Organizational behavior
    Organizational change
    Organizational learning
    Organizational sociology
    Curricula

McKendall, M. (1993). The tyranny of change: Organizational development revisited. *Journal of Business Ethics*, *12*(2), pp. 93-104.

The premise of this paper is that planned organizational change, commonly known as organizational development, induces compliance and conformity in organizational members and thereby increases the power of management. These consequences occur because organizational development efforts create uncertainty, interfere with the informal organization, reinforce the position of management, and further entrench management purposes. These consequences occur regardless of the intentions of management and regardless of whether the goals of the organizational development intervention were achieved. Instead of examining these consequences, practitioners and theorists have engaged in self-deception and depoliticized the practice of induced organizational change by creating a field known as Organizational Development.

Subject Terms:

> Organizational change
> Organizational behavior
> Management
> Industrial sociology
> Industrial relations
> Organizational structure
> Industrial organization
> Organizational sociology
> Personnel management
> Corporations
> Moral & ethical aspects

McManus, K. (2012). The six o'clock sweet spot. *Industrial Engineer: IE*, *44*(1), pp. 20.

The article discusses workplace performance improvement related to the starting of daily work processes. The author connects such processes to the daily routine of adjusting a shower's temperature to one's personal liking. He explains that lost startup time should be mitigated, as diversified customer expectations often require organizations to frequently change.

Subject Terms:

Job performance
Organizational change
Process control
Production planning

McMorland, J., & Erakovic, L. (2011). Governance in a not-for-profit: The 'Am Calon' case. *University of Auckland Business Review*, *13*(1), pp. 5-11.

The article examines the principles of governance applied by not-for-profit (NFP) organizations in New Zealand. It discusses the story of NFP organization 'Am Calon' to reflect the critical issues of organizational development that challenge principles and practices of governance. It presents an integrated set of principles linking developmental stages of organizational structure to the members of the organization as a whole.

Subject Terms:

    Nonprofit organizations
    Organizational governance
    Organizational change
    Organizational behavior
    Management

Meyer, S. (2004). Organizational response to conflict: Future conflict and work outcomes. *Social Work Research*, *28*(3), pp. 183-190.

The purpose of this study was to examine how an organization's response to conflict affected the amount and intensity of future conflict and negative work outcomes. In this cross-sectional study of 3,374 government service workers, bivariate correlations and multiple regressions revealed associations between managers' conflict-handling style (CHS) and indicators of productivity and conflict ratings. As managers' use of the forcing CHS increased, the rate of accidents, absenteeism, and overtime increased. However, a path analysis showed that the relationship between CHSs and negative work indicators disappeared when the amount and intensity of conflict was held constant. Implications for social work are discussed.

Subject Terms:

    Conflict Management
    Employer-Employee Relations
    Workplace Violence

Milburn, J. (2009). Finding truth in outliers. *OD Practitioner*, *41*(1), pp. 32-37.

The article explores assumptions and methods for handling superfluous or rogue data. Rogue data is defined as of-the-record data. In doing so, the article investigates what organizational development (OD) practitioners do when they are required to pursue something that is outside of the common themes. It looks into how the OD consultants deal with confidential information that is shared with them from a single source that surfaces during the course of client work but does not fall into common themes, or that conventional theory says one should not pursue.

Subject Terms:

    Organizational change
    Confident communications
    Professional ethics
    Business communication
    Organizational sociology
    Disclosure of information
    Truthfulness & falsehood

Miller, F. A., & Katz, J. H. (2010). Riders on the waves of change two people, one black and one white, discuss their journeys through an era of struggle, opportunity and world change. *OD Practitioner, 42*(2), pp. 37-42.

A narrative is presented which explores the author's experience of being the partners to an organization development-consulting firm to open an opportunity for change.

Subject Terms:

Organizational change

Minahan, M. (2010). OD and HR. *OD Practitioner*, *42*(4), pp. 17-22.

The article discusses the underlying issues whether organization development (OD) function be imbedded within the human resource (HR) or stand independently in the organization. It features the stands of several central thinkers and scholars on the issue. It also states the connection between the HR and OD function, how HR influence OD function, and their differences. The disadvantages of being independent along with the tips that OD practitioners must consider are further cited.

Subject Terms:

> Organizational change
> Personnel departments
> Labor discipline
> Performance – Management
> Employment practices
> Research personnel

Mintzberg, H. (2011). From management development to organization development with impact. *OD Practitioner*, *43*(3), pp. 25-29.

The article discusses the development of the Impact program and how this program can be used to improve development of and in organizations. It explores how the program was born, which is defined as a pact between learning program manager and the group he/she assigns back at work for management development. It states that the Impact program, which acts on the International Masters in Practicing Management (IMPM), includes several components to promote it.

Subject Terms:

Organizational change
Executive -- Training of
Assessment centers (Personnel management procedure)
Organizational learning
Industrial management

Mohr, B. J., Saint, D., & Millar, P. (2011). What is appreciative governance? *AI Practitioner*, *13*(4), pp. 13-22.

This article defines Appreciative Governance (AG), offers a comparison with current organizational practices and provides a detailed description of the purpose of governance and how AG responds to and accomplishes that purpose.

Subject Terms:

  Organizational change
  Organizational behavior
  Corporate culture
  Communication in organizations
  Organizational learning
  Leadership
  Organizational structure
  Corporate governance

Monette, M. L., & Vogelsang, J. (2011, Winter). International OD practices and challenges. *OD Practioner, 43*(1), pp. 4-5.

The article discusses various articles published within the issue, including one by Therese Yaeger and Peter Sorensen on the global role of organizational development, one by John Conbere and Alla Heorhiadi on the Socio-Economic Approach to Management (SEAM), and one by Billy Desmond on an effective group development model.

Morgan, H., & Jardin, D. (2010). HR + OD = Integrated Talent Management. *OD Practitioner, 42*(4), pp. 23-29.

The article discusses the implications of the human resource (HR) and organization development (OD) domains as a guide for HR and OD leaders towards the betterment of their respective organizations. It cites the overlap between HR and OD practitioners in relation to practicing talent management. It notes the interrelated practices involved in integrated talent management (ITM) and lists several questions that HR and OD should consider. Conceptual models of ITM are also presented.

Subject Terms:

    Personnel management
    Organizational change
    Personnel departments
    Industrial management
    Human capital
    Management

Morgeson, F. P., & Hofmann, D. A. (1999). The structures and functions of collective constructs: Implications for multilevel corporations and theory development. *Academy of Management Review, 24*(2), pp. 249-265.

The authors address gaps in the multilevel organizational theory development literature by critically examining the structure and function of collective constructs. Structure emerges from interaction and can, over time, come to influence systems of interaction. Functions represent the causal outputs of constructs and provide a mechanism for integrating constructs across levels. The authors then discuss implications arising from this perspective and present a set of guidelines for multilevel research and theory development.

Subject Terms:

    Organizational sociology
    Organizational
    Organizational change
    Data analysis
    Regression analysis
    Corporate culture
    Organizational behavior
    Multilevel models (Statistics)
    Guidelines
    Typology (Psychology)

Morrill, C. (1991). Conflict Management, honor, and organizational change. *American Journal of Sociology*, *97*(3), pp. 585.

How do top managers of a large American corporation manage conflict among themselves? This article investigates intra-corporate executive conflict management in a Fortune 500 manufacturer via ethnographic methods. It focuses on the links between executive conflict management and widespread innovations in (1) top managerial formal structure and (2) hostile takeovers and their symbolic imagery. More specifically, the article focuses on how these innovations disrupted the traditional social structure and "rules of the game" among top managers. The resulting new "culture of honor" suggests several implications for the study of managerial uncertainty, inertia, accountability, and control in contemporary American corporations.

Subject Terms:

Conflict management
Organizational change
Social structure
Ethnology
Problem solving

Morris, T. (2007). Internal and external source of organizational change: Corporate form and the banking industry. *Sociological Quarterly*, *48*(1), pp. 119-140.

How do internal and external constraints impact the likelihood that organizations enact organizational change? Resource dependence theory argues that organizational change is a response to internal and external constraints. However, the interaction of these constraints remains theoretically and empirically under considered. Using longitudinal data from the U.S. banking industry, I examine this question from a resource dependence perspective and I also incorporate explanations from transaction cost economics, organizational ecology, and institutional theoretical perspectives. I find that external constraints limit the impact of internal constraints on organizational change. I explore how this finding fits within resource dependence theory.

Subject Terms:

Organizational change
Organizational behavior
Externalities (Economics)
Organizational structure
Business models
Transaction costs

Morrison, J. L. (2003). Organizational change for corporate sustainability: A guide for leaders and change agents of the future (Book). *Journal of Education for Business*, *79*(2), pp. 124-125.

Reviews the book "Organizational Change for Corporate Sustainability--A Guide for Leaders and Change Agents for the Future," by Dexter Dunphy, Andrew Griffiths and Suzanne Benn.

Subject Terms:

　　　Organizational change

Murrell, K. L. (2004). Hope: Our intended OD legacy for 2050. *Organization Development Journal*, *22*(2), pp. 21-28.

Offers thoughts on what is desired as legacy in the practice of organization development (OD). Visions for a future that will make OD work more meaningful and show what OD practitioners are capable of leaving as legacy in a field moving into its second half of its first century of development.

Subject Terms:

> Organizational change
> Organizational behavior
> Organization
> Management

Murrell, K. L. (2007). Nature's way of teaching us about change: Learning from hurricanes, tsunamis, earthquakes and other natural disasters. *Organization Development Journal*, *25*(1), pp. 27-36.

Our field of Organization Development is challenged to respond to human needs at not only the individual and organizational level but at the societal level as well. In this challenge is the potential to renew our field and expand its positive impact. Discussed in this paper is the recent set of natural and manmade disasters and what the field of O.D. can bring to these in terms of help and understanding. The case to be made is very personal to the author in that much of the changes he has had to deal with were forced on him by the recent Gulf Coast hurricanes. What is offered here is a perspective on change work where external influences were near total and the response in terms of O.D. was only possible from a position of vulnerability and not from any senior consulting or leadership position.

Subject Terms:

> Organizational change
> Natural disasters
> Tsunami

Murrell, K. L., & Sanzgiri, J. (2011). OD practice: Rediscovering our international roots. *Organization Development Journal*, *29*(4), pp. 53-65.

Since its inception, the field of Organizational Development has directly been involved in global transformational change. To the end the field continues to expand into new cultures, new settings; and investigates, analyzes and assimilates new styles and novel approaches to organizational dilemmas. Through its history, OD has benefited from dedicated professionals who continue to contribute throughout their lives. Some of the most important contributions in the globalized world are that these professionals have chosen to live in other cultures and yet continue their thoughtful practice and research. Their ongoing contributions expand and deepen our knowledge and understanding of new practices. In this setting of a fast moving and growing field, we define four-core values common to and deep set within the field of OD; these are meant as a starting point, a proposed definition for further discussion and refinement. Through these core values, we bring the history of OD and current and past practitioners' dedication to the field into a realm that looks forward to what effects we would like OD to have on the world now and in the future. In particular, the focus is on the progressive humanity, improved sustainability, and advancement of intercultural sharing and appreciation.

Subject Terms:

> Organizational change
> Corporate culture
> Organizational ideology
> Organizational behavior
> Organizational structure
> Business ethics

Narayanan, V. K., Colwell, K., & Douglas, F. L. (2009). Building organizational and scientific platforms in the pharmaceutical industry: A process perspective on the development of dynamic capabilities. *British Journal of Management*, *20*(1), pp. 25-40.

In this paper, we examine the process of dynamic capability development in a large pharmaceutical firm. Using interviews with multiple managers at different organizational levels, we developed two narratives of the process of developing two separate dynamic capabilities in the same firm. We focus on three areas that prior research has shown to be critical in the early stages of the process of implementing new strategic initiatives: the cognitive orientations of key personnel, managerial action undertaken within the firm, and the firm's internal and external contexts. We provide evidence that managers undertake specific initiatives based on their own particular cognitive orientations, and that senior managers play a major role in the development of capabilities by imprinting the organization with their specific cognitive orientation and then orchestrating the multilevel organizational routines necessary for actualization of a capability. These replicable actions by senior management during the early stages of capability development can lead to the development of a capability that is not initially in the cognitive frames of lower level employees. Finally, we will show that internal and external contingencies have a profound impact on the decision to develop a capability, and to discontinue its development. Our findings thus suggest that the process of developing new capabilities shares common elements with other strategic initiatives.

Subject Terms:

> Strategic planning
> Industrial management
> Management science
> Executive ability (Management)
> Competitive advantage
> Empirical research
> Decision-making
> Business development
> Senior leadership teams
> Business planning
> Comparative studies

Nathan, J. D., & Whatley, A. (2006). Critical theory: A means for transforming organization development. *Organization Development Journal*, *24*(2), pp. 61-68.

There has been a paradigm shift in higher education and in the corporate world regarding Organization Development (O.D.). Historically, O.D. and managerial capitalism focused on valuing people as much as profit. This ethic transformed into financial capitalism: a market-driven mindset resulting in global corporate migration to find the cheapest labor and resources, maximizing shareholder value. The practice disregards human considerations while focusing on financial considerations. Critical Theory (CT) can be instrumental in reversing this trend by bringing a return to a humanistic orientation in the workplace.

Subject Terms:

> Organizational change
> Organizational research
> Human capital
> Personnel management
> Economic structure
> Work environment

Nekoranec, W. (2009). Ethical leadership and OD practice. *OD Practitioner, 41*(2), pp. 2-7.

The article discusses the impact of ethical leadership in addressing the economic situation in the U.S. It examines the contribution of an ethical leadership to the success of companies, determines how chief executive officers (CEO) acted in tough situations, and reflects the ways on how companies endured the economic situation. It highlights the research on the ethical leadership of the CEOs, and discusses how they maintain the support and influence in the organization development (OD). It provides insights on working with an ethical leadership in a given situation and within an organization.

Subject Terms:

Leadership
Chief executive officers
Organizational change
Business planning
Organizational structure
Corporation – Growth
Management
Executive ability (Management)

Neumann, J. (2006). Building O.D.C. as an academic discipline: An international perspective. *Organization Development Journal*, *24*(3), pp. 114-115.

The article discusses the establishment of the organizational development and change as an academic discipline in international perspectives. The author points out those organizational communities and their change-related practitioners are hungry for research-based guidance during challenging times. He adds that organizational studies departments that had been incorporated into business schools find themselves competing.

Subject Terms:

Business education
Organizational behavior
Universities & college
Organizational change
Organizational learning
Organizational sociology
Curricula

Neumann, Y., & Finaly-Neumann, E. (1994). Management strategy, the CEOs cognitive style and organizational growth/decline: A framework for understanding enrolment change in private colleges. *Journal of Educational Administration, 32*(4), pp. 66-66.

A model is developed that links organizational growth and decline to competitive strategy, the strategy -making process, and the personal characteristics of the chief executive officer (CEO). The model is tested empirically for private liberal arts colleges where the size of the student enrollment is a dominant factor for the vitality of the institution. The major findings of the study are that: 1. enrollment growth is associated with a focused strategy, the CEO innovation style, differentiation and assertive strategy -making process, and 2. the major discriminating factors between institutions experiencing enrollment growth and those experiencing enrollment decline are a focused strategy and the CEO innovator cognitive style.

Subject Terms:

> Management styles
> Strategic planning
> Enrollments
> Cognition & reasoning
> Effects
> Corporate growth
> Models

Nielsen, L. (2012). Quantifying qualitative OD results. *OD Practitioner*, *44*(1), pp. 38-43.

The article offers the author's views on the issue concerning organization development (OD) and the ways on how to raise the credibility of OD professionals. It notes that OD is perceived in the business world as a soft skill such as a teamwork tool, a communication, and a conflict resolution and is not recognized by top executives as a source of cost-reduction and revenue generation. It mentions that quantitative hard data is essential in raising the credibility of OD professionals.

Subject Terms:

Organizational change
Team in the workplace
Communication in organizations
Conflict management
Executives
Cost control
Business revenue
Change agents

Nistelrooij, A. v., & Siminia, H. (2010). Organization development: What's actually happening? *Journal of Change Management, 10*(4), pp. 407-420.

A great deal of commentary and controversy about the state of organization development (OD) has to do with a lack of clarity regarding what it is about organizations that can be affected by an OD effort. Recent initiatives suggest that a new set of OD practices are emerging based on a social constructionist orientation. With this in mind, this article aims to contribute to a theoretical understanding of what it is about organizations that can change, based on Berger and Luckmann's (1966) social constructionist framework. It describes three distinct change processes that take place because of OD interventions. The article ends with a discussion of some of the implications for OD practice, specifically with regard to 'programming' dialogue as the main vehicle for change.

Subject Terms:

> Change
> Organizational change
> Social change
> Organization
> Social constructionism
> Social processes

Noer, D. M. (1997). How we can make our leaders more effective. *Management Review*, *86*(1), pp. 24.

Presents an excerpt from the book `Breaking Free: A Prescription for Personal and Organizational Change.'

Nutt, P. C. (2004). Organizational de-development. *Journal of Management Studies, 41*(7), pp. 1083-1103.

Organizational decline prompts leaders to downsize, reducing the size of the workforce in an attempt to cut costs. This paper discusses some of the dangers of downsizing in which organizations experience an unanticipated and unwanted loss of core competencies. An alternative to downsizing is offered, showing how organizations can 'de-develop' by slowly and deliberately moving to a lower order of organized complexity, retaining essential core competencies and supporting functions. To produce a 'soft-landing' that preserves core competencies, a new identity is forged and connections to the new identity are uncovered. The connections point out what must be preserved, such as a crucial channel for key products, for the new identity to survive and flourish. The de-developed organization preserves customers, products, markets, channels, revenue sources, alliances, skilled people, ways to organize, and/or image crucial to the new strategic identity before letting go of the remaining customers, products, etc. The paper identifies conditions under which de-development can be desirable and suggests a 'devolutionary' process that points out some of the key moves needed to reduce organized complexity and realize a soft landing.

Subject Terms:

> Downsizing of organizations
> Business failures
> Industrial costs
> Core competencies
> Organizational change
> Industrial organization
> Organizational behavior
> Complex organizations
> Change management
> Strategic planning
> Decentralization in management

Oakerson, R. J., & Parks, R. B. (2011, Feb). The study of local public economies: Multi-organizational, multi-level institutional analysis and development. *Policy Studies Journal, 39*(1), pp. 147-167.

One important extension of the IAD framework has been to the study of local public economies. These are multi-organizational, multi-level arrangements defined as the set of governmental jurisdictions, public and nonprofit agencies, and private firms that interact in various patterns to provide and produce public goods and services within a specific locality or region. Commonly, the localities or regions studied from this perspective have been U.S. metropolitan areas, often defined as a central city and its surrounding or adjoining county. Localities can be delineated, however, on various terms, and in the IAD framework, it is the geo-physical nature of a locality that, in substantial part, drives the analysis. One of the strengths of the approach is its capacity to explain local variations in public organization as a function of the geo-physical diversity of localities, while at the same time developing empirical generalizations and normative principles that apply across diverse regions. What, for example, might the organization and governance of a complex metropolitan area have in common with the organization and governance of a complex protected area, such as the greater Yellowstone eco-region or the Adirondack Park? Construing both sorts of regions as local public economies can enhance our overall understanding of public organization at the same time that it permits a more nuanced understanding of diverse localities. Such work contributes to the ongoing IAD project of 'understanding institutional diversity.'

Subject Terms:

> Macroeconomics
> Research
> Nonprofit sector
> Multilevel models (Statistics)
> Public institutions

O'Neil, D. A., & Sharp, E. (2009). Hit or miss? Assessing the fit between learning objectives in OD&C graduate programs and organizational requirements for OD&C practitioners. *Organization Development Journal*, *27*(2), pp. 69-83.

This research examined the degree of fit between academic learning objectives of graduate programs in Organization Development and Change and organizational hiring requirements for OD&C practitioners using content and thematic analyses. Results suggest that OD job postings are heavily focused on training and development and people management components. In contrast, components more frequently noted on OD graduate program web sites are people management, organizational analysis and design, human resource functions (specifically change management), execution, and lastly training and development. This suggests that the people management focus is well placed, but that there may be a disconnect between what OD hiring managers are seeking and the curriculum focus of graduate programs in OD regarding training and development components. Directions for future research and ways to continue to address the practitioner-academic gap are offered.

Subject Terms:

> Organizational change
> Organizational effectiveness
> Change management
> Organizational structure
> University & colleges
> Personnel management
> Organizational behavior
> Organizational research
> Graduate work
> Organizational aims & objectives

Oreg, S. (2006). Personality, context, and resistance to organizational change. *European Journal of Workand Organizational Psychology, 15*(1), pp. 73-101.

The article proposes and tests a model of resistance to organizational change. Contrary to most works on resistance, resistance was conceptualized here as a multifaceted construct. Relationships among resistance components and employees' personalities, the organizational context, and several work-related outcomes were examined.

Oswick, C., Grant, D., Marshak, R. J., & Cox, J. W. (2010, Mar.). Organizational discourse and change: Positions, perspectives, progress, and prospects. *Journal of Applied Bahavioral Science, 46*(1), pp. 8-15.

The article discusses various studies published within the issue, including one by Frank Mueller, Olga Suhomlinova and Andrea Whittle concerning the discursive methods used by change agents to facilitate change, one by Eli Teram about the impact and consequences of organizational change and one by Christopher Anne Easley on the need for different awareness on the researchers' part.

Pádár, K., Pataki, B., & Sebestyén, Z. (2011). A comparative analysis of stakeholders and role theories in project management and change management. *International Journal of Management Cases*, *13*(4), pp. 252-260.

This paper analyses the similarities and differences between the stakeholder and role concepts, which are in current use in project management and change management literature. The similarities are noticeable at first sight but it is not clear where the domains of the different definitions of the two management disciplines overlap and where they vary from each other significantly. We have not found such an interdisciplinary comparison in the literature of the two fields. At first, we compared the widely used definitions of project, first order (or morphostatic) and second order (or morphogenetic) change to find the overlapping areas where it is reasonable to compare the different role definitions at all. We found an overlapping area where the different role definitions are all valid and the role theories can be compared. The typical project stakeholders are project sponsor, project manager, project management team, project team, influencers, customer/user, performing organization etc. The typical change roles are sponsor (initiating and sustaining), agent, target, advocate, facilitator etc. We found sameness's, similarities and differences alike between the two sets of roles. The most important conclusion is that the findings enable participants working on these types of activities to rely on both bodies of knowledge properly.

Subject Terms:

> Project management
> Change management
> Organizational change
> Management
> Role theory

Paghaleh, M. J. (2011). Organizational innovation and research & development. *International Journal of Business & Social Science, 2*(13), pp. 245-249.

Today, such countries can enter international competition that is always seeking to use new technologies and this can be possible only with research and development center (R & D) in accordance with the criteria for active and new world. These centers According to the aim of creation, Have different policies. In this paper, after reviewing the literature, will investigate and explain the success factors of research and development, Position of research and development in advanced countries and Iran. Then compare them. At the end, solutions for improving researches are provided.

Palm, Mary E,M.S.N., R.N., & Nelson, Margaret A,M.S.N., R.N. (2000).
Leadership development course for creating a learning environment. *The
Journal of Continuing Education in Nursing, 31*(4), pp. 163-168.

The purpose of the meetings was to identify the components of an educational plan
for the development of new skills that would best prepare leadership to promote the
cultural changes desired in the system. The purpose of this activity is to help people
make the distinction between learning as the structured, academic, intentional event
of school, to which everyone easily relates, and the spontaneous, natural learning
that occurs in everyone's life as an integral part of being in the world. Others
identify class concepts that they have been able to employ, for example, changing
the way they evaluate employee "fit" and hiring someone for what they can learn.
Others report simple changes in vocabulary and approach to communication, using
expressions such as "let's explore that" to encourage bi-directional information
sharing.

Pandey, M. (2012). Change though painful yet all embrace: A case study. *BVIMR Management Edge*, *5*(1), pp. 20-26.

Change can be seen as inevitable and constant, unpredictable and sometimes alarming and yet to stand still risks decay and stagnation. Only those organizations will prosper in the long run which are adaptive and willing to change according to the environmental demands and is ready to make changes of their own to adjust to the new realities of competition. It is with this capability and quest to compete, two of world's renowned scientific research institutes in India namely CMRI and CFRI have been merged to form a new entity CIMFR. This paper attempts to examine the various issues relating to change management process in these two Institutes. The purpose of this research is to examine the factors affecting change interventions and organizational learning. For the purpose of study, non-directive interviews were conducted to get insights about the effect of change on employees. Findings indicate that for an effective transition from an old order to new, a proper well-devised people strategy is necessary.

Subject Terms:

> Competition (Economics)
> Research
> Organizational learning
> Organizational change
> Change management
> Research institutes

Pandey, S., & Sharma, R. K. (2011). Organization development interventions for prospectors: A theoretical framework and its empirical validation. *Global Business & Management Research*, 3(1), pp. 79-95.

Purpose - Organizational Development (OD) interventions facilitate and transform a prospector firm to become more adaptable, responsive and innovation directed. In this paper, we propose a theoretical framework that suggests some specific OD interventions suitable for prospectors. Methodology - We carry out a Meta - synthesis of 20 case studies and find good support for this framework. OD interventions include talent management, trans-organizational development, virtual team, high involvement design and flexible job design. OD interventions and cases studies are taken from published and unpublished sources. A standard procedure was used to ensure the rigor of the synthesis. Contradictory evidence is collected to consider the action hypothesis. Findings - A Meta -schedule was prepared after the qualitative evaluation of the cases. This schedule is compared with the prospector firm's problem -solution choices. We found OD interventions, effectively improving prospector's strategic position. Results showed how interventions in the study improved efficiency, integration capacity and uncertainty redressal in the turbulent times. The study describes the role of organizational development interventions in 'between the firm learning', trust building and mutual adaptation. Originality/value - The present study is one of the early attempts to link organization development intervention with business strategy. The empirical evidence based synthesis provides 'ready to choose' option for practitioners. It offers holistic view of context by combining individual, primary data based qualitative studies.

Subject Terms:

    Organizational change
    Strategic planning
    Business planning
    Business development
    Methodology

Author-Supplied Keywords:

    Flexible Job Design
    High Performance Organization
    OD Intervention
    Prospector
    Talent Management
    Trans-organizational Development
    Virtual Team

Parsch, J. H., & Baughman, M. (2010). Towards healthy organizations: The use of organization development in academic libraries. *Journal of Academic Librarianship*, *36*(1), pp. 3-19.

Two surveys assess use of organization development (OD) in Association of Research Libraries. Analysis presents organizational, deans' and staff professionals' perspectives on OD use. The study is the first broad analysis of academic library OD use and supports the concept of the "healthy organization."

Subject Terms:

> Organizational behavior
> Organizational change
> Academic libraries – Administration – Employee participation
> Library employees
> Customer services
> Academic libraries – Administration
> Academic library directors
> Training
> Library public services

Parsons, B. (2009). Evaluative inquiry for complex times. *OD Practitioner*, *41*(1), pp. 44-49.

The article offers a look at an evaluative inquiry process. When the process is implemented as specified, it enhances the ability of the organization to respond more flexibly to changing conditions than relying only on goal setting and strategic planning processes. The article describes how and why the process works, which is intended to help the readers adapt the approach for the contexts in which they work. The process is developed at a community college through a grant from the of the U.S. National Science Foundation. Building an evaluative inquiry process into creates an ongoing strategy for renewal and success.

Subject Terms:

     Organizational change
     Goal setting in personnel management
     Strategic planning
     Organizational accountability
     Personnel management
     Community colleges

Patten Jr., T. H. (1994). Ho'oponopono: A cross-cultural model for organizational development and change. *International Journal of Organizational Analysis (1993 - 2002), 2*(3), pp. 252.

Is organization development (OD) culture-bound to American and western applied behavior science or exportable? There is evidence that one concept and set of techniques (called ho'oponopono), which was developed in ancient Hawaii but are still practiced today, have close parallels to OD techniques in conflict management used by pace-setting American corporations. Ho'oponopono is apparently culturally transferable. Thus, OD has been uniquely addressed in a culture far removed from urban-industrial America and is, with minor adaptations, applicable to contemporary corporations. Perhaps OD-and certainly at least the ho'oponopono methodology for conflict management –can be made culturally fungible. The paper concludes with an explanation of how this transferability can made in ho'oponopono.

Subject Terms:

    Organizational change
Conflict management

Patwell, B., Gray, D., & Kanellakos, S. (2012). Discovering the magic of culture shifts. *OD Practitioner*, *44*(1), pp. 11-17.

A case study is presented on organizational change initiatives aimed at helping the organization development (OD) professionals in promoting and managing successful change initiatives. This study took place in the City of Ottawa, Ontario. It notes that the study aimed at motivating every city employee to adopt the practices of Services Excellence (SE), to develop leaders and managers, and to create a positive environment for change. It mentions that the study reveals that culture change occurs because of a series of small shifts among stakeholders.

Subject Terms:

> Case studies
> Organizational change
> Executives
> Stakeholders
> Change agents

Pellegrinelli, S., & Webster, R. (2011). Multi-paradigmatic perspectives on a business transformation program. *Project Management Journal*, *42*(6), pp. 4-19.

The study of projects and programs, and their management, is seen as becoming an increasingly vibrant and pluralistic academic field, having transcended its pragmatic and functionalist roots. Drawing upon Burrell and Morgan's () four paradigms of sociological research, we briefly review research that is set within each paradigm. This plurality of perspectives has informed and sensitized our analysis and sense making of a major business transformation program within a European retail bank. This article presents key findings and insights from our inductive research. The research adds to our knowledge and understanding of program-based transformational change and depth, richness, and perspectives useful to practitioners.

Subject Terms:

>   Organizational change
>   Change management
>   Project management
>   Research banking

Pellettiere, V. (2006). Organization self-assessment to determine the readiness and risk for a planned change. *Organization Development Journal, 24*(4), pp. 38-43.

The rapid pace of change in today's competitive environment creates pressure within the organization to implement change initiatives in order to meet the demands of its stakeholders. A plethora of organizational change initiatives and strategies have been attempted to meet these pressures but their success rate in achieving their objectives has been less than satisfactory. Studies have shown that approximately 70% of organizational change initiatives fail. One of the main causes for these failures is the lack of a thorough diagnostic investigation in an organization's readiness and risk for a planned change. A thorough diagnostic investigation includes both an external and internal analysis using some form of an assessment to determine the need to change as well as its readiness and risk in making the planned change. Organizations have a tendency not to conduct a thorough internal analysis and have a propensity to initiate quick-fix solutions when implementing a change initiative.

Subject Terms:

    Capitalist & financiers
    Stakeholders
    Organizational change
    Organizational structure
    Personnel changes
    Job enrichment
    Adaptability (Psychology)

Peluso, D. (2010). Compete, coordinate, collaborate. *OD Practitioner*, *42*(4), pp. 40-46.

The article discusses the strategies and learnings acquired when establishing OD functions in each company. It illustrates how a company's OD function varies its work from HR. It features case studies on OD within the line operations in financial services and manufacturing along with their corresponding diagrams. It also accounts the partnership of OD and HR, which hosted a conference on change management, online collaboration, and performance improvement.

Subject Terms:

    Organizational effectiveness
    Organizational change
    Business enterprises
    Organization charts
    Conferences & conventions
    Personnel management

Petrick, J. A. (1992). Organizational ethics development: Implications for human resource professionals. *Journal of Education for Business*, *67*(6), pp. 330.

Discusses the organization ethics development and the implications they hold for resource professionals. Survey of key literature; Fear and manipulation are the primary moral strategies used for survival; Next level of moral development is Machiavellianism; Recent research concerning the moral development of American business professionals and business graduate students; Research methodology and findings.

Subject Terms:

Business Ethics

Pettingrew, A., Woodman, R., & Cameron, K. (2001, Aug.). Studying organizational change and development: Challenges for future research . *Academy of Management Journal, 44*(4), pp. 697-713.

This article presents several studies that examine organizational change. The author notes that certain issues should be addressed when examining the studies. This should include an examination of the multiple contexts; levels of analysis in studying organizational change; the inclusion of time; history; process and action; the link between change processes; and organizational performance; the investigation of international and cross-cultural comparisons; the study of receptivity customization; sequencing; pace and episodic versus continuous change; and the partnership between scholars and practitioners in studying change. The author discuss how these issues are related to the concepts in the studies and note they research has not addressed these issues now.

Pfeffer, J. (1996). Why today's leaders need the lessons of the past. *Leader to Leader*, (2), pp. 36-41.

The article focuses on the importance of peeping into the history of organizational development for building up an effective organization. In the search for new and trendy, organizations fail to appreciate the strengths as well as the weaknesses of past organizational arrangements. Therefore, ignorance of the history of the evolution of organizations and employment relations makes an organization prone to remake old mistakes. Leaders can gain three benefits from a deeper understanding of history: first, a fresh perspective from seeing that what looks new is really old; second, a fuller appreciation of the hidden costs of these allegedly new arrangements; and third, an understanding of the appropriate steps to sustain competitive advantage and avoid being swept up in fads and fashion.

Subject Terms:

Organizational change
Organization
Organizational behavior
Organizational structure
Corporate reorganizations
Workforce planning

Piotrowski, C. (2006). Supplemental databases for researchers and practitioners in organization development. *Organization Development Journal*, *24*(2), pp. 101-102.

This paper discusses the utility in implementing a multi-database strategy when striving to achieve comprehensive coverage on research topics in organization development. The author expands on the earlier work of Piotrowski and Armstrong (2004, 2005) that stressed the use of the major databases in the O.D. field, i.e., PsycINFO and ABI/INFORM. By relying on supplemental online databases, in a research retrieval strategy, researchers increase the probability of obtaining comprehensive literature reviews on select topics in the field.

Subject Terms:

    Organizational research
    Organizational change
    Business planning
    Online databases
    Organizational behavior
    Organizational sociology

Piotrowski, C., & Armstrong, T. R. (2004). The research literature in organization development: Recent trends and current directions. *Organization Development Journal*, *22*(2), pp. 48-54.

This article focuses on research literature in organization development (OD). Finding of an analysis of major topical areas in OD from 1992-2003 identifying the most popular topical areas in OD scholarly literature including organizational change, international/cultural applications and team building.

Subject Terms:

Organizational change
Organizational behavior
Organizational structure
Organization

Piotrowski, C., & Armstrong, T. R. (2005). Major research areas in organization development: An analysis of ABI/INFORM. *Organization Development Journal*, *23*(4), pp. 86-91.

This study examined trends on popular research areas indexed in the business online database ABI/INFORM Global. A comparison to the findings of an earlier study published in the Organization Development Journal by Piotrowski and Armstrong (2004), which reported on a bibliographic analysis of the database PsycINFO, was the main focus. Results indicated that several topical areas (e.g., OD change, transformational change, OD theory, international issues) are the most cited subjects in both ABI/INFORM and PsycINFO. Other topics (e.g., leadership, strategic planning, and technology) showed divergent research output as a function of database used. The authors caution both researchers and practitioners about the unique features of online databases and suggest the use of a 'multi-database' strategy when conducting comprehensive literature reviews.

Subject Terms:

> Online databases
> Organizational change
> Strategic planning
> Technology
> ABI/INFORM (Information retrieval system)

Plager, D. (2009). Action "Thinking". *OD Practitioner*, *41*(1), pp. 38-43.

The article provides the organizational development (OD) practitioners with an overview of action learning. In doing so, it takes an in-depth look into action learning from a cognitive perspective to see why it works and provide recommendations for ways to maximize the effectiveness of action learning as an OD tool. The article delves into the cognitive components that underlie the supposition that by following the action learning process, individual participants develop greater leadership skills. The author proposes that exploring the cognitive strategies used in action learning will demonstrate how those strategies can develop and enhance leadership behaviors and competencies.

Subject Terms:

    Organizational change
    Organizational effectiveness
    Industrial efficiency
    Organizational sociology
    Active learning
    Industrial development

Pledger, C. (2007). Building manager effectiveness by combining leadership training and organization development. *Organization Development Journal, 25*(2), pp. 71-76.

How can training and organization development be combined to improve individual manager and team effectiveness? How can lessons from the classroom be sustained and reinforced? At Goldman Sachs University, we designed an experiential learning program that uses the same models to achieve three goals: (1) build critical managerial skills at the individual level, (2) improve team performance at the group level, and (3) provide follow-up Organization Development interventions to further improve individual and team effectiveness.

Subject Terms:

> Leadership
> Training
> Organizational change
> Organizational behavior
> Research
> Executive ability (Management)
> Collaborative learning
> Experiential learning
> Learning
> Cognitive learning

Popov, E. (2011). Institutional atlas. *Atlantic Economic Journal, 39*(4), pp. 445-446.

The article focuses on the development of institutional atlas. It says that the multifactorial, hierarchical system characteristics of economic institutions are ordered by four criteria, which are the fields of activity, place of occurrence, management functions, and manufacturing roles. It explains the difference between formal and informal institutions. It also discusses the similarity of norms within the organization consisting of a set of formal and informal groups.

Subject Terms:

    Organizational change
    Production management
    Hierarchies
    Social institutions
    Social norms
    Social groups

Porod, C. H. (2010). Trends in the evolution of international organization development. *Organization Development Journal, 28*(4), pp. 91-108.

Since the first publication of the Organization Development Journal in 1983, the emergence of internationally focused articles has been a key feature in the diffusion of knowledge among readers. Throughout its 28-year span, approximately every issue published has contained research about the application and progress of International OD. With time, however, the presence of international articles has continued a rollercoaster-like trend (see Table 1). This article provides a glance into the impact of International OD over time as seen in the ODJ.

Subject Terms:

> Economic trends
> Popular culture
> Organizational change
> Consumer preferences
> Organizational behavior
> International cooperation
> Individual preferences
> Economic aspects

Porras, J. I., & Silvers, R. C. (1991). Organizational development and transformation. *Annual Review of Psychology, 42*(1), pp. 51-78.

This article reviews recent research that improves our understanding of planned change theory and practice. The author proposes a new model of the change process rooted in a conception of organizations presented by Porras (1987) and Porras et al (1990). This change model organizes our understanding of the field and guides the discussion of research presented in the second half of the chapter.

Preston, J. (2011). Letter from the editor. *Organization Development Journal*, *29*(4), pp. 5.

An introduction is presented in which the editor discusses various reports within the issue on topics including cultural assessment tool in a small franchise restaurant, family-owned business succession, and industry performance during disasters.

Subject Terms:

Corporate culture
Chain restaurants
Family-owned business enterprises

Prywes, Y. (2011). Organization history. *OD Practitioner*, *43*(2), pp. 40-45.

The article explains how not understanding the history of an organization influences change efforts. It discusses how this history acknowledges the importance of a contextual approach advocated by systems thinkers that find value in putting organizational change into the context of a larger whole. It also examines how historical perspective complements most organizations to change theories, which tend to focus on the link between the present and desired future state.

Subject Terms:

    Organizational change
    Change management
    Organizational sociology
    Organizational effectiveness
    Organizational aims & objectives

Purser, R. E. (2011). Developing awareness of time in organizational change. *Organization Development Journal, 29*(1), pp. 45-62.

Turbulence is experienced as an external force bearing down on us – a force whose pace and power we cannot seem to control or change. Rather than simply accepting turbulence as a social given, this paper argues that the roots of societal, organizational, and personal problems are related to the fact that we have become estranged and alienated from time. This paper examines how conventional organizational change assumptions and certain "avante garde" approaches are shaped by a linear temporal order, which is inherently limiting. A new vision of time is explored, along with a new approach for generating and embodying transformative knowledge, which has implications for our personal and organizational lives.

Subject Terms:

    Organizational change
    Social change
    Time -- Sociological aspects
    Inquiry (Theory of knowledge)
    Transformative learning

Quattronea, P., & Hopperb, T. (2001). What does organizational change mean? Speculations on a taken for granted category. *Management Accounting Research, 12*, pp. 403-435.

Despite widespread research on why and how organizations change, what constitutes change is often taken for granted. Its definition is avoided. Studies based on individuals' rational choice imply that change flows from purposive actions in accordance with an objective, external reality whereas contextualism argues that change results from institutional pressures, isomorphism and routines. However, both depict change as the passage of an entity, whether an organization or accounting practices, from one identifiable and unique status to another. Despite their differences over whether reality is independent, concrete and external, or socially constructed, both assume that actors (or researchers) can identify a reality to trace the scale and direction of changes. This reflects modernist beliefs that organizational space and time are unique and linear. The paper takes issue with this and argues that 'a-centered organizations' and 'drift' should replace conventional definitions of organizations and change. The arguments are inspired by the arguments of the sociology of translation and constructivism, and insights from two case studies of Enterprise Resource Planning system implementations in large multinational organizations. The latter illustrate how defining change is problematic—as new systems gave rise to multiple spaces and times within the organizations. The paper traces the implications of this for control and accounting studies *tout court*.

Subject Terms:

ERP
SAP
Organizational change
A-centred organization
Sociology of translation
Constructivism

Ramos, M. C., & Chelster, M. A. (1010, Spring). Reflection on a cross-cultural partnership in multicultural orgabnizational development efforts. *OD Practioner, 42*(2), pp. 4-9.

The article discusses the authors' view on the cross-cultural partnership in multicultural organizational development in the U.S. The authors explain human interactions and organizational behavior to the long-term partnership as activist practitioners and generators of scholarship. They discuss the development and dynamics of our own cross-cultural partnership in race, gender and professional orientation.

Ramos, M. C., & Rees, C. J. (2008). The current state of organization development: Organizational perspectives from Western Europe. *Organization Development Journal*, *26*(4), pp. 67-80.

The paper highlights various perspectives that have been offered about the current state of Organization Development (O.D.) and then proceeds to explore an additional perspective, namely, how O.D. as a management activity is described and located by organizations, which employ O.D. practitioners. In order to address this issue, an analysis was undertaken of the recruitment and selection literature associated with 30 advertised vacancies for O.D.-related positions in Belgium, Spain and the UK. The findings reveal the extent of the overlap between O.D. and HR activities in these organizations. The findings also reveal wide variations in the activities that the organizations associate with an O.D. role and the skills and competencies they require from O.D. practitioners. Finally, the study highlights the extent to which organizations in different cultural contexts require different skills and competencies from the internal O.D. practitioners they employ.

Subject Terms:

> Organizational change
> Organizational behavior
> Personnel management
> Advertising, Recruitment
> Employee selection
> Literature

Rampersad, H. K. (2004). Learning and unlearning in accordance with organizational change. *Organization Development Journal, 22*(4), pp. 43-60.

Organizational change is a learning process. Changing oneself can occur after learning new things and unlearning others. Individual learning must then be converted into collective learning, leading ultimately to organizational change. This article introduces a new change management model and checklists that facilitate this learning process and benefit the durability of organizational changes. It is based on Total Performance Scorecard; Redefining Management to Achieve Performance with Integrity, Butterworth-Heinemann Business Books, 2003.

Subject Terms:

    Organizational change
    Organizational structure
    Corporate turnarounds
    Management
    Organizational behavior
    Learning

Redding, C. J. (2004). Increasing accountability. *Organization Development Journal*, *22*(1), pp. 56-66.

This article offers advice to organization development (OD) practitioners on how to increase accountability in ways that liberate people or dominate them. The article also presents common experiences in performance management.

Subject Terms:

> Personnel management
> Organizational change
> Management
> Organizational behavior
> Organizational sociology
> Corporate culture

Reinardy, S. (2010). Downsizing effects on personnel: The case of layoff survivors in US newspapers. *Journal of Media Business Studies*, *7*(4), pp. 1-19.

Lewin's (1947) organizational development theory says that after an organization reorganizes and downsizes, it "refreezes" to pre-change comfort levels. This study of 2,159 newspaper layoff survivors indicates they perceive that refreezing at this time would be problematic because it would result in a journalism of mediocrity, more focused on quantity rather than quality. In light of previous research, the reduction of newsroom staff also alters the product attributes. In this case it may perpetuate the downward spiral of lost circulation and advertising revenue. The results indicate that for those employees experiencing a decline in trust, morale, satisfaction and commitment, newspapers are creating production-line journalism that is seen as void of purpose and function.

Subject Terms:

      Downsizing of organizations
      Mass media – Employees
      Layoffs
      Communication
      Mass media industry
      Audiovisual materials industry
      Publisher & publishing
      Broadcasting industry
      Psychological aspects

Ridge, R. (2005, Jul). A dynamic duo: Staff development and you. *Nursing Management, 36*(7), pp. 28-35.

To meet the demands of an increasingly complex and aging patient population, implement a comprehensive framework for staff development.

Subject Terms:

Staff Development

Ridley, C. W. (1993). Putting organizational effectiveness into practice: The preeminent consultation task. *Journal of Counseling & Development, 72*(2), pp. 168-177.

Successful consultation relies on the consultant's ability to conceptualize the operations of the total organization, an overview of the theoretical and practical applications of the construct "organizational effectiveness" (OE) is presented in relation to consultation. Barriers limiting earlier conceptualizations and applications of the construct are identified and discussed. A model of OE that melds open systems, organizational, and consultation theories is presented as a tool for guiding maximally beneficial consultation interventions. The implications of this model for consultation practice, advancing theory and research, and professional ethics are discussed.

Subject Terms:

Organizational effectiveness
Counseling
Counselor
Professional ethics
Psychology

Ríos, D. (2010). Renuncio. *OD Practitioner*, *42*(2), pp. 19-24.

A personal narrative is presented which explores the author's experience of being an agent of cultural change in Organization Development (OD) in the U.S.

Subject Terms:

   Social change

Robertson, P. J., & Seneviratne, S. J. (1995). Outcomes of planned organizational change in the public sector: A meta-analytic comparison to the. *Public Administration Review*, *55*(6), pp. 547.

This article focuses on the outcomes of planned organization change in public sector. Although the potential benefits of planned organizational change for public organizations seem apparent, previous literature pertinent to this issue is more equivocal. On the one hand, literature-discussing differences between public and private organizational development may not be as viable in the public sector. Because private sector organizations are driven primarily by market or consumer preferences, organizational effectiveness is more readily measured in terms of efficiency and profitability. As a result, change activity can be implemented and assessed using these narrow criteria as the primary basis for evaluating their success, possibly making it easier for these change efforts to be successful. The above arguments are based on the premise that there are clear-cut and consistent differences between organizations in the public and private sectors that is that these generalizations hold true for most public organizations.

Subject Terms:

    Organizational change
    Associations, institutions, etc.
    Private sector
    Nonprofit organizations
    Public sector
    Industrial efficiency
    Break-even analysis

Robertson, R. R. (1997). Walking the talk: Organizational modeling and commitment to youth and staff development. *Child Welfare, 76*(5), pp. 577-589.

Notes that effective staff development and positive youth development practice share many philosophical and structural similarities. The article examines the relationship between youth and staff development and the long-term implications of organizational commitment to the youth-serving movement's newest paradigm-positive youth development.

Robison, B. (2006). Building O.D.C. as an academic discipline: A qualitative inquiry into a maturing field of organization development. *Organization Development Journal, 24*(3), pp. 107.

The article discusses the most influential field of organizational development and change as an academic discipline. The author interviewed 11 individuals who influential in the field including Billie Alban, Chris Argyris, Robert Golembiewski, John Kotter, and others. The author argues that a theoretical base was developed in the study, indicating that traditional and newer fields and occupations can and have become professions.

Subject Terms:

    Organizational change
    Professional

Rogers, K., & Hudson, B. (2011). The triple bottom line: The synergies of transformative perceptions and practices for sustainability. *OD Practioner, 43*(4), pp. 3-9.

The article discusses aspects of sustainability and the concept of the triple bottom line. It explains the ideas and drivers behind sustainability in which the concept has come to revolve around organizational development and the triple bottom line (TBL) with three elements, the social, economic, and environmental components of sustainable practices. Also explored are the harmonies in the three elements of TBL in the issue of climate change, natural capitalism, and environmental protection.

Romme, A. L. (2011, Mar.). Organizational development interventions: An artifaction perceptive. *Journal of Applied Behavioral Science, 47*(1), pp. 8-32.

Given the highly instrumental nature of the literature on organizational interventions, this article explores and defines key elements of an artifaction theory of organizational development (OD) interventions. Four dimensions of artifaction are distinguished: ascription, fabrication, displacement, and reinterpretation. This framework then serves to develop a number of propositions regarding the nature and background of OD interventions, the ability to create alternative purposes and values, the involvement of stakeholders in the intervention process, the deliberate incompleteness of the intervention approach adopted, as well as its standardization and codification. Finally, the article discusses how an artifaction perspective on OD intervention may serve to develop an OD science that is theoretically as well as practically significant.

Romme, A. L., & Damen, I. C. (2007, Mar). Toward science-based design in organization development. *Journal of Applied Behavioral Science, 43*(1), pp. 108-121.

Herbert Simon once suggested that the social sciences are actually the hard sciences due to the enormous complexity and interconnectedness of the elements within social systems. This insight is also critical in understanding the nature of change and development of large organizational systems. Adopting a science-based design approach, the authors place emphasis on the importance of developing construction principles and design rules for the implementation of large-scale organization development (OD) interventions. The empirical part of the article draws on several case studies of OD projects that employ the methods of circular redesign. The first case illustrates how implementation may fail because of a lack of awareness of the complexity of OD implementation and experimentation processes. The second case suggests that a coherent set of principles and rules can provide a common framework and language for scholars, managers, and consultants working together in large-scale organizational change projects.

Subject Terms:

    Organization development
    Science-based design
    Design rules
    Codification

Rosenberg, R. (2003). The eight rings of organizational influence™ How to structure your organization for successful change. *Journal for Quality & Participation, 26*(2), pp. 30-34.

The article discusses strategies to implement organizational change in business enterprises. Tips to improve focus in the workplace; Factors to consider to maintain the balance in the organizational structure of a company; Importance of learning to for employee and organizational development.

Subject Terms:

Organizational change
Business enterprises
Organizational structure
Industrial organization
Work environment
Organizational behavior

Rothwell, W. J., & Sullivan, R. (2005). *Practicing Organizational Development: A Guide for Consultants* (2nd ed.). San Fransisco, Ca: Pfeiffer.

Organization Development (OD) is about planned change. As change turned into the only consultant, many managers and other people are pursuing changes strategies with vigor. OD is a major strategy for leading and managing change at the individual, group, intergroup, organizational, interorganizational, and large systems levels. This book is about to be an effective change manager, change leader and OD consultant.

Subject Terms:

    Organizational change
    Management
    Business consultants
    Handbooks, manuals

Royal, C., & Vogelsang, J. (2010). From the editors. *OD Practitioner, 42*(2), pp. 1.

Howard Jackson, Quandrant Behavior Theory approach by Cathy Royal and destruction to gender oppression by John Jenkins, presents an introduction to the journal in which the editor discusses the model for culture change.

Subject Terms:

    Organizational change
    Social change

Rubery, J., Earnshaw, J., Marchington, M., Cooke, F., & Vincent, S. (2002). Changing organizational forms and the employment relationship. *Journal of Management Studies, 39*(5), pp. 645-672.

This paper draws upon new research in the UK into the relationship between changing organizational forms and the reshaping of work in order to consider the changing nature of the employment relationship. The development of more complex organizational forms - such as cross organization networking, partnerships, alliances, use of external agencies for core as well as peripheral activities, multi-employer sites and the blurring of public/private sector divide has implications for both the legal and the socially constituted nature of the employment relationship. The notion of a clearly denned employer-employee relationship becomes difficult to uphold under conditions where employees are working in project teams or on-site beside employees from other organizations, where responsibilities for performance and for health and safety are not clearly defined, or involve more than one organization. This blurring of the relationship affects not only legal responsibilities, grievance and disciplinary issues and the extent of transparency and equity in employment conditions, but also the definition, constitution and implementation of the employment contract defined in psychological and social terms. Do employees perceive their responsibilities at work to lie with the direct employer or with the wider enterprise or network organization? And do these perceptions affect, for example, how work is managed and carried out and how far learning and incremental knowledge at work is integrated in the development of the production or service process? So far the investigation of both conflicts and complementarities in the workplace has focused primarily on the dynamic interactions between the single employer and that organization's employees. The development of simultaneously more fragmented and more networked organizational forms raises new issues of how to understand potential conflicts and contradictions around the 'employer' dimension to the employment relationship in addition to more widely recognized conflicts located on the employer-employee axis.

Subject Terms:

    Complex organizations
    Organizational sociology
    Industrial relations
    Strategic alliances (Business)
    Business networks
    Partnership (Business)
    Organizational structure
    Employees
    Work environment
    Superior subordinate relationship
    Psychology

Rutledge, M. (2009). Sense making as a tool in working with complexity. *OD Practitioner*, *41*(2), pp. 19-24.

The article discusses the significance of sense making in an organization. It explores the eight features of sense making and examines how the organization development (OD) practitioner will learn from the sense making process. It analyzes the result of the qualitative research study on sense making which indicates the importance of the process to the group members, and suggests how practitioners can assist client groups by reflecting back to themselves. It outlines the advantages of sense making since as it lead the group into discovery, and identifies the differences between sense making and dialogue.

Subject Terms:

    Knowledge management
    Organizational behavior
    Organizational change
    Communication
    Research
    Management
    Teams in the workplace
    Corporations – Growth
    Sense making theory (Communication)
    Methodology

Salter, N. P., & Varney, G. H. (2008). A comparative analysis of program content for the 2007 OD network and the AOM-ODC division conferences. *Organization Development Journal*, *26*(4), pp. 33-42.

The article reports on the comparative study of Academy of Management Organizational Development and Change Division (AOM-ODC) Annual Conference and Organizational Development Network (ODN) Annual Conference in the U.S. As stated, the AOM is an academic forum and ODN is a practitioner forum. It also mentions that the academic community centers on inquiry and research into how organizations work with much research being conducted in organizations while practitioners seldom rely on academic research instead they formulate experience based theories without testing them for their validity. In addition, both academics and practitioners add to the lack of communication between each other.

Subject Terms:

> Conferences & conventions
> Research
> Communication
> Organizational change
> Comparative studies
> Forums (Discussion & debate)
> Inquiry (Theory of knowledge)
> Experience

Sanzgiri, J., & Gottlieb, J. Z. (1992). Philosophic and pragmatic influences on the practice of organization development, 1950-2000. *Organizational Dynamics*, *21*(2), pp. 57-69.

This article discusses information on philosophical and practical influences on the organizational development (OD) in the U.S. The field has evolved through a number of phases from 1950s to 1980s and the change will expected to continue. In the early stages (1950s and 1960s), the major developers of this concept for this era such as Warren Bennis, Chris Argyris, and Edgar Schein had spoken about the social philosophy or normative goal of OD. For the future practice of OD there needs to be an increasingly sophisticated acceptance of divergent positions. OD practitioners will assist organizations in rethinking their hierarchical structures and the distribution of power.

Subject Terms:

> Organizational change
> Organizational behavior
> Influence (Psychology)
> Social sciences – Philosophy

Saraiva, H. (2011). The balanced scorecard: The evolution of the concept and its effects on change in organizational management. *EBS Review*, (28), pp. 53-66.

This paper presents a history of the Balanced Scorecard concept from its earliest appearance to the present day, showing that its evolution is closely related to the fact that the concept has always had a practical application. This article's aim is to establish a relationship between its applications as an instrument and the evolution of the Balanced Scorecard concept; it also seeks to demonstrate that this concept has induced changes in the way that organizational management at the global level has evolved in recent years due to its innovation and wide spread use around the world. These objectives are pursued through a review of literature and texts published by the authors of the concept and other relevant contributors.

Subject Terms:

Balanced scorecard (Management)
Organizational change
Industrial management
Innovations in business
Organizational performance

Sauder, M., & Espeland, W. (2009). The discipline of rankings: Tight coupling and organizational change. *American Sociological Review*, *74*(1), pp. 63-82.

This article demonstrates the value of Foucault's conception of discipline for understanding organizational responses to rankings. Using a case study of law schools, we explain why rankings have permeated law schools so extensively and why these organizations have been unable to buffer these institutional pressures. Foucault's depiction of two important processes, surveillance and normalization, show how rankings change perceptions of legal education through both coercive and seductive means. This approach advances organizational theory by highlighting conditions that affect the prevalence and effectiveness of buffering. Decoupling is not determined solely by the external enforcement of institutional pressures or the capacity of organizational actors to buffer or hide some activities. Members' tendency to internalize these pressures, to become self-disciplining, is also salient. Internalization is fostered by the anxiety that rankings produce, by their allure for the administrators who try to manipulate them, and by the resistance they provoke. Rankings are just one example of the public measures of performance that are becoming increasingly influential in many institutional environments, and understanding how organizations respond to these measures is a crucial task for scholars.

Subject Terms:

Discipline
Organizational behavior
Organizational change
College students
Self-control
Internalization
Social pressure
Institutional theory (Sociology)
Social learning
Stress (Psychology)
Rating of
Law schools
Performance standards

Schein, E. H. (1993). Legitimating clinical research in the study of organizational culture. *Journal of Counseling & Development, 71*(6), pp. 703-708.

In this article, the author argues that the traditional research paradigm used in industrial-organizational psychology is not useful in understanding the deeper dynamics of organizations, especially those phenomena that we label as "cultural." The use of data obtained during clinical and consulting work should be legitimated as valid research data. The clinical model is spelled out and illustrated in the study of organizational culture.

Subject Terms:

Culture
Organization
Research
Psychology
Mental health consultation

Schein, E. H. (2010). The role of organization development in the human resource function. *OD Practitioner*, *42*(4), pp. 6-11.

The article discusses the connection between the area of organization development (OD) and human resource (HR). It notes the five essential trends, which influence both HR and OD including complexity of subcultures and cultural diversity, as well as evolution of information technology. An overview of the history of OD and HR along with the basic roles of HR managers is presented. It also focuses on the preliminary conclusion and issues on the change in social values between company and employee.

Subject Terms:

    Personnel management
    Organizational change
    Industrial management
    Goal setting in personnel management
    Industrial relations

Schifo, R. (2004). OD in ten words or less: Adding lightness to the definitions of organizational development. *Organization Development Journal, 22*(3), pp. 69-80.

Some of the greatest minds in organization development (OD) have expended considerable energy trying to define their profession. While there is wisdom in each of these definitions, their primary audience appears to be other OD practitioners. Since there seem to be few OD definitions that are brief, yet capture the essence of OD, this article offers ground rules and develops a methodology for creating one. Its target audience is those outside of the OD profession.

Subject Terms:

Organizational change
Management
Organization
Organizational sociology

Schifo, R. (2007). Electric utility achieves business results through organizational development. *Organization Development Journal, 25*(4), pp. 135-140.

Central Vermont Public Service (CVPS) is traded on the NYSE and is subject to the same legal requirements imposed on much larger organizations. Yet its modest size enables it to make decisions more quickly, making it a unique laboratory for organizational development (OD) intervention. CVPS's executive team has made OD a focal point of its talent management strategy. This decision was driven by pressure to meet rising customer expectations, at lower cost with a stretched workforce, and in anticipation of a talent shortage. As a result, OD has contributed significantly to achieving desired business results.

Subject Terms:

Electric utilities
Organizational change
Financial performance
Business planning
Change management
Strategic planning
Management
Organizational effectiveness

Schmid, G., Schütz, H., & Speckesser, S. (1999). Broadening the scope of benchmarking: Radar charts and employment systems. *LABOR: Review of Labor Economics & Industrial Relations*, *13*(4), pp. 879.

Abstract. Over the last few years, 'benchmarking' advanced to a key word in organizational development and change management. Originally, a tool in business studies to search for best practice that led to superior performance, increasingly benchmarking also became practice in non-profit and public institutions. Notably, the European Commission uses benchmarking as an instrument to monitor its employment guidelines. The radar chart approach is one of a number of special analytical tools that has been developed in this connection. The paper discusses the advantages and limits of benchmarking labor market performance by radar charts, recommends a broadening of the scope by using the employment systems approach and provides, in both cases, examples of application.

Subject Terms:

  Benchmarking (Management)
  Organizational change
  Labor market

Schulz, K., & Geithner, S. (2010). Individual and organizational development as interplay: An activity oriented approach. *Zeitschrift Für Personalforschung, 24*(2), pp. 130-151.

We see the contribution of our paper as discussing an integral perspective of individual and collective development. Considering learning and development, we suggest a conceptual orientation on activity theory (Chaiklin/Hedegaard/Jensen 1999; Engeström 1987, 2001, 2005). Therefore, we see the workplace as a context where people learn through collective acting and reflecting. According to Engeström we consider learning as expansive development which is brought about through contradictions in daily work and the need to change mindsets. We will refer to two case studies in medium sized firms in the technology and automotive supply industry in Germany. Using qualitative methods of social research (participatory observation, interviews, data analysis), we have analyzed the work and learning activity of production systems. We have described the current demands of the inherent contradictions in the operational work activity. Furthermore, we describe contradictions between the requirements of work and the actual learning methods. Based on these results we develop a platform model of collaborative learning and development.

Subject Terms:

> Organizational change
> Work environment
> Automobile industry
> Individual development
> Activity coefficients

Searcy, D. L. (2012). Unleashing lean's potential, one behavior at a time. *Strategic Finance*, *93*(7), pp. 41-45.

The article discusses lean production strategy. A discussion of how and why two sister companies were successful in changing their organizational culture to welcome innovation and in implementing lean strategies is presented. Topics include the five lean success layers, improvements from lean implementation at each company, and definitions of lean manufacturing terms.

Subject Terms:

Lean manufacturing
Corporate culture
Organizational change
Strategic planning
Change agents
Success

Seidman, A. N. (2011). Listening for the sacred within - and at work. *OD Practitioner*, *43*(3), pp. 36-43.

The article offers the author's insights on the relationship between spirit direction (SD) and organization development (OD). The author notes that SD attends to the spiritual formation of an individual devoting the practice of OD in an organization and enhances the performance of members. She cites Nancy Smith's proposed factors that lead to spirituality at work movement like an ethical breakdown in corporations. She adds that spiritual discernment at work is practiced in spiritual direction.

Subject Terms:

Organizational change
Job performance
Business ethics
Spiritual direction
Spiritual formation
Spirituality
Discernment of spirits

Seidman, W., & McCauley, M. (2009, Summer). A scientific model for grassroots O.D. *Organizational Development Journal, 27*(2), pp. 27-37.

The biggest challenge for most Organizational Development (O.D.) cultural change initiatives is to get large numbers of people to quickly and completely embrace a desired change. Grassroots O.D. engages many people quickly while still supporting executive initiatives. By integrating research on positive deviance, fair process, neuroscience and mass customization into a practical methodology, a grassroots approach to O.D. can change organizations' cultures faster, more predictably and more completely than was previously thought possible.

Subject Terms:

> Organizational change
> Organizational growth
> Organizational effectiveness
> Organizational structure
> Organizational planning
> Management
> Organizational research
> Organizational sociology

Seidman, W., & McCauley, M. (2011). Transformational leadership in a transactional world. *OD Practitioner*, *43*(2), pp. 46-51

The article addresses an issue that impedes the success of optometrist, the dominance of transactional thinking in organizations and the negative impact that transactional thinking has on organizational performance improvement. It provides a detailed checklist and strong financial incentives to achieve the required operational results. It also offers a means of making transformational leadership a reality in organizations.

Subject Terms:

    Organizational effectiveness
    Organizational change
    Transaction analysis
    Transformational leadership

Seiling, J. (2004). An approach to writing. *Organization Development Journal*, *22*(1), pp. 107-110.

This article offers advice on creative writing in the field of organization development. Characteristics of articles written for journals with cross sections of readers; Reference in designing context for writing; Need for writers to overcome "the writer's block".

Subject Terms:

> Organizational change
> Organizational behavior
> Corporate culture
> Creative writing
> Creation (Literary, artistic, etc.)

Sharkey, L. D. (2006). ODC division - 21st century reflection on O.D. and its relevance to the workplace. *Organization Development Journal, 24*(4), pp. 17-20.

This paper, based largely on the author's experience in various human resources roles, outlines the critical link between organization development and organizational change. Integral to this interface are the issues of facilitation, leadership development, team building, and assimilation. O.D. and change are indispensable to the adaptability of modern organizations to emerging challenges in the business environment. O.D. practitioners have a central function in meeting this challenge.

Subject Terms:

> Personnel management
> Organizational behavior
> Organizational change
> Organization
> Management
> Organizational structure
> Personnel changes
> Job enrichment
> Adaptability (Psychology)

Sharma, D. (2009, Fall). Faboulous facilitator: MARVELous origins of the OD superhero. *Organizational Development Journal, 27*(3), pp. 35-52.

The article focuses on the significance of superhero metaphor in the workplace. It discusses the relationship between comics and organizational development. The author claims that the superhero metaphor in comics, in turn, can serve, as a useful tool to empower workers and the superhero metaphor in the workplace appears to have more value in the hands of individual leaders. Furthermore, the paper delves into the metaphor of the superhero itself and analyzes the metaphor in terms of its usefulness for individuals within organizations.

Shepard, K. (2004). Letters to the organization development journal. *Organization Development Journal, 22*(1), pp. 116-119.

The author asserts that the future of organization development (OD) depends on selecting leadership with sufficient capability. Analysis on Elliott Jaques' concepts of levels of work; Findings of a study by the Corporate Leadership Council which concluded that there is no career path for OD professionals; Author's experience with a strategic planning effort for a human resource professional association in Canada.

Subject Terms:

Organizational behavior
Management
Corporate culture
Organizational change

Šimanskienė, L. (2005). The research on opinions and needs for learning and developing in Lithuanian organizations. *Knowledge-Based Economy: Management of Creation & Development*, pp. 339-350.

The article focuses on research, which defines opinions and needs for learning and developing in Lithuanian organizations. Intelligent organizations are organizations that learn while knowledge-based organizations are organizations that rely on cognitive rather than physical activities. Organizational development is a change approach that focuses on changing the attitudes and behaviors of organizational members. Learning organizations are defined as organizations where people continually expand their capacity to create the results they desire.

Subject Terms:

    Organizational learning
    Organizational change
    Knowledge management
    Organizational behavior

Simpson, M. J. (2005). Aligning human resources/organizational development with internal client needs: A transportation metaphor. *Organization Development Journal*, *23*(1), pp. 68-72.

To achieve their mission, Human Resource/Organizational Development (HR/OD) professionals need to form an alliance with internal clients, especially at the senior level, because they can elect to use HR/OD services, or not, and demand that HR/OD professionals prove themselves before partnering with them. This expectation makes it important for HR/OD professionals to differentiate types of internal clients, adopt the most appropriate response style with each, and align in the best way with each style.

Subject Terms:

> Personnel management
> Organizational change
> Industrial management
> Human capital
> Transpiration
> Labor supply

Smith, F., Wright, A., & Huo, Y. (2008). Scapegoating only works of the herd is big: downsizing, management turnover, and company turnover. *Journal of International Business Strategy*, *8*(3), pp. 72-83.

The field of academic study on corporate strategy is still in its juvenile stage. Owing to its multidisciplinary nature, this vein of research has been influenced by different streams of academic literature in social sciences. Scholars in economics, finance, marketing, organizational studies (behavior, theory, and development), and communications all claim some impact on the field of strategy research. Other disciplines, such as industrial psychology, sociology, political science, and anthropology, have also offered useful theoretical models that help to advance the research on strategic management. Within the field of business policy and strategy, the antecedents and consequences of strategic change are increasingly the targets of academic research. In essence, change has become the name of the survival game in today's business world due to globalization, shortened technology cycles, shifting demographics, and fast-changing expectations among workers and customers. The greater the external forces for change, the greater the competitive pressure, the greater is the internal demand for change (Beatty & Ulrich, 1991). Even slower growth or slipping market share, while still showing a profit, can become a call for change. The result of strategic change is, however, not always positive. Under tremendous pressure to improve the financial performance -- caused especially by the decline of the stock price -- the board of directors may make hasty, ill-conceived personnel changes, and top management may make imprudent strategic decisions. It is therefore no surprise that, in the history of corporate America, successful turnarounds have occurred less frequently than downward spirals. This paper will explore the relationship between two of the strategic alternatives commonly undertaken by financially stressed companies, downsizing and top management turnover, and the subsequent probability of a successful turnaround. In the past a wide variety of qualitative data sources, such as case studies, management consultants, and biographies of CEOs, have been used by researchers for empirical studies of strategic change. We see the need to conduct a more rigorous quantitative analysis of publicly traded firms across a broad range of industries.

Subject Terms:

Downsizing of organizations
Organizational change
Corporate reorganizations
Corporate turnarounds
Industrial management
Strategic planning

Sorensen, P. F., & Yaeger, T. F. (2006). Building O.D.C as an academic discipline: A program director's perspective. *Organization Development Journal, 24*(3), pp. 106.

The article discusses the comments of the authors about organizational development and change in five themes. The author points out five themes on organizational development and change, which include the overall state of organizational development, it changes, its setting agenda, the role of doctoral programs, and how these academic programs are effective.

Subject Terms:

Organizational change
Organizational behavior
Organizational sociology
Organizational structure
Organizational commitment

Sorensen, P. F., Yaeger, T. F., Savall, H., Zardet, V., Bonnet, M., & Peron, M. (2010). A review of two major global and international approaches to organizational change: SEAM and appreciative inquiry. *Organization Development Journal*, *28*(4), pp. 31-39.

In this article, we review and compare two major approaches to Organization Development, one of French origin, the Socio Economic Approach to Management (SEAM); the second of U.S. origin - Appreciative Inquiry (AI). Both of these change approaches have significant global and international applications. The article reviews their origins, processes, the role of research, and discusses major differences and contributions to the field of OD.

Subject Terms:

> Organizational change
> Change management
> Economic development -- Sociological aspects
> Strategic planning
> Adoption of ideas
> Modernization (Social science)

Starkweather, H. (2010). Embodied differences. *OD Practitioner*, *42*(1), pp. 39-43.

The article examines the significance of disability and Queer Theory for organization development (OD) in helping invisible minorities in organizations. It states that the cultural norms and biases that hinder groups and contribute able normativity in the workplace can be highlighted when Queer Theory and disability are combined. It adds that practitioners can guide their clients to appreciate the complexity of all individuals by understanding the Queer Theory's performative nature of identity.

Subject Terms:

> Discrimination in employment
> Organizational change
> Organizational behavior
> Work environment
> Clients
> Queer theory
> Discrimination against people with disabilities
> Social norms

Starr, L. (2006). Building O.D.C. as an academic discipline: A program director's perspective. *Organization Development Journal, 24*(3), pp. 108-109.

The article provides tips and guidelines on building organizational development and change as an academic discipline. The author relates that he was invited by the Philadelphia College of Osteopathic Medicine to create a Master of Science in Organizational Development and Leadership degree program. The curriculum hired the faculty designed and directed the marketing including the website, established the student and faculty policies, and launched the program in November 2001 with 15 students.

Subject Terms:

Universities & colleges
Organizational change
Organizational learning
Organizational sociology
Organizational behavior
Curricula

Stock-Kupperman, G. (2011). Towards an identification of core sources in organizational development using doctoral dissertation. *Journal of Management Policy & Practice, 12*(4), pp. 104-112.

Researchers in organization development have used practitioner opinions in determining core sources in the field, which take a qualitative rather than a quantitative approach. Library and information science has a history of identifying core sources through citation analysis. This study has borrowed that methodology to develop a core list of sources utilized by researchers in the field. In this study, citations from 118 theses from three doctoral programs in organization development and behavior were analyzed to determine these core sources. The result of this investigation produced a quantitatively derived list of core sources as a starting point for further research.

Subject Terms:

> Organizational change
> Library science
> Information science
> Academic dissertations
> Doctoral degree

Stone, F. (1995). Overcoming opposition to organizational change. *Supervisory Management, 40*(10), pp. 9.

Provides tips for managers on how to overcome staff resistance to change. Monitoring of events within the organization for preparation for change that comes; Seeking of change when it can be positive; Role modeling of a positive attitude; Confrontation of feelings; Selling of the need for change; Setting of small goals; Involvement of staff in planning for change.

Subject Terms:

Organizational change
Management

Stragalas, N. (2010). Improving change implementation. *OD Practitioner, 42*(1), pp. 31-38.

The article focuses on the change implementation model that corporate management must provide to their employees using the John Kotter framework. The Kotter model shows that managers must be positive and offer proactive explanations to illustrate the connection between new approaches and improved organizational performance. The article adds that implementation can be improved and percentage of successful change initiatives can be successful if there is a proactive approach to change management.

Subject Terms:

> Change management
> Organizational change
> Organizational behavior
> Industrial management
> Employees – Attitudes

Strudy, A., & Grey, C. (2003). Beneath and beyond organizational change management: Exploring alternatives. *Organization Articles, 10*(4), pp. 651-661.

This essay introduces contributions to a special issue exploring alternative accounts of organizational change management (OCM). It begins with identifying why such alternatives are needed by pointing to core assumptions within OCM, including a practical and ontological prochange bias, managerialism and universalism. The alternatives to OCM are then framed in terms of the constructionism associated with various forms of discourse analysis. It is argued that the contributions show, both theoretically and empirically, the limitations of OCM as conventionally understood.

Subject Terms:

    Organizational change
    Organizational structure
    Management

Sulamoyo, D. (2010). "I Am Because We Are": Ubuntu as a cultural strategy for OD and change in Sub-Saharan Africa. *Organization Development Journal*, *28*(4), pp. 41-51

This article explores the concept of Ubuntu as a cultural philosophy and way of life in Africa that has an influence on OD strategies for change and development. Ubuntu is a philosophical thought system that defines Africa's humanistic way of defining life through others. According to Mangaliso (2001, p. 24): Ubuntu can be defined as humaneness - a pervasive spirit of caring and community, harmony and hospitality, respect and responsiveness - that individuals and groups display for one another. Ubuntu is the foundation for the basic values that manifest themselves in the ways African people think and behave toward each other and everyone else they encounter. How are OD and Ubuntu connected from a basis of values? How can Ubuntu are integrated into African organizations as means of facilitating change? In order to understand Ubuntu in the context of organizational change and development, the article will first explore the Global Organization Development and the African culture to provide the framework.

Subject Terms:

> Organizational change
> Strategic planning
> Change management
> Economic development – Sociological aspects
> Adaptation of ideas
> Modernization (Social science)

Sulamoyo, D. (2010). Building beyond already established OD success rates: An interview with Dr. Robert T. Golembiewski, RODC. *Organization Development Journal*, *28*(4), pp. 11-19.

An interview with author, editor and University of Georgia (UG) professor Robert T. Golembiewski is presented. When asked about his history with the Organization Development (OD) Institute, he claims that he got himself involved in the field back in 42 years when he and Donald Cole ran across into each other. He stresses that recognizing the fact that the types of organization development designs are not being differentiated well is important.

Subject Terms:

Interviews
Editors
Organizational change
College teachers

Sutton, R. F. (2009). Happiness for the pragmatic optimist and everyone else. *OD Practitioner, 41*(4), pp. 51-56.

The article focuses on the proposed measurements of employee happiness, which can change organizational development issues. It cites that the engagement of employees where they agreed that interaction with coworkers are always mostly positive, feel challenged, and do not take work home. Ed Powers, organizational designer, suggested that Organizational Design (OD) must focus on human factors including wellbeing and wellness, emotional and physical health, and motivation and empowerment.

Subject Terms:

> Employees – Attitudes
> Organizational change
> Organizational structure
> Organizational
> Job satisfaction
> Social aspects

Sweem, S. (2010). Fall back or spring forward: Is it time for a new HR/OD alliance? *OD Practitioner*, *42*(4), pp. 30-35.

The article discusses the impact of the collaboration between the organizational development (OD) and human resource (HR), the HR strategic business partner model, to an organization. It states that the combination of both HR and OD paves to the emergence of human resource organizational effectiveness (HROE) professional. An overview of the historical perspective of HR and OD is presented. It also focuses on the move of several organizations to utilize the strategic business partner model.

Subject Terms:

> Organizational effectiveness
> Organizational change
> Competitive advantage
> Strategic alliances (Business)
> Strategic planning

Than, L., & Lao, T. M. (2010). Evidence on efforts to align organizational structure and business strategies. *Global Journal of Business Research (GJBR)*, 4(1), pp. 71-84.

This paper is based upon a research study to determine the significance of managerial leadership practices in a corporation's transformation during the period from 2004 to 2008. The study attempted to discover how managerial leadership practices effectively advance horizontal integration of an inclusive and collaborative organization. The study was grounded on propositions involving organizational development roles, IT governance, and collaborative organizations. Triangulated inquiry from peer-reviewed documents and a survey of 24 participants who included 2 women and 22 men comprising a chief information officer, seven functional managers, eight project managers, and eight engineers of a corporation in the Northeastern United States confirmed the propositions. The findings indicated that horizontal integration has begun in transition from being separate toward becoming collaborative. This paper will reveal how the Full Spectrum Leadership model involving collaborative and integrative leadership practices could enhance disparate images that are subculture bound.

Subject Terms:

> Information technology
> Management
> Business planning
> Organizational behavior
> Horizontal integration
> Project management

Thompson, C. (2011). The nonprofit organizational model. *OD Practitioner*, *43*(2), pp. 34-39.

The article describes the nonprofit organizational model with examples of how it can be used for goal setting, organizational analysis and strategic planning. It reveals the purpose of the model, which is to break down the complexity of an organization into manageable pieces to focus on important organizational elements. It also explains each aspect of the model.

Subject Terms:

        Nonprofit organizations
        Organizational goals
        Organizational change
        Complex organizations
        Organizational effectiveness

Torres, S. (2007). Organizational development: From public relations nightmare to competitive edge. *Organization Development Journal, 25*(4), pp. 151-155.

The article compares the implementation of organizational development (OD) plans of two companies, a financial institution and a healthcare company ARAMARK Corp. The financial institution as a part of its OD redesigned its annual report to highlight employees who had received awards for outstanding work. It informs that its readers met the report with strong opposition as it valued the employees more than the economic growth. ARAMARK changed its culture as a part of its OD to help hospitals enhance patient care. ARAMARK allows its support services clients to select an OD component as part of their contractual agreement.

Subject Terms:

> Organizational change
> Financial institutions
> Corporation reports
> Medical care
> Performance awards
> Corporate culture
> Support services (Management)
> Customer services

Trullen, J., & Barunek, J. M. (2007, Mar). What a design approach offers to organization development. *Journal of Applied Behavioral Science, 43*(1), pp. 23-40.

In this article, the authors describe characteristics of design science as a type of organization development (OD) intervention and as an approach to actionable theorizing. The authors discuss ways that design science approaches are typically but not necessarily consistent with OD's values as well as the types of intervention motors they typically use. That is, they often reflect humanistic values, but they need not necessarily do so. Design science typically uses action research and participation intervention motors but does not include as much self-reflection as is the case in much OD work. Design approaches focus much more on action than do most current OD interventions; thus, they add an important dimension to OD practice. In addition, they suggest ways of linking this focus on action with hypothesis testing and theorizing more than do most current OD interventions. Thus, they offer the possibility of revitalizing OD.

Subject Terms:

    Organizational change
    Organizational behavior
    Organizational design

Tyrrall, D., & Parker, D. (2005). Fragmentation of a railway: A study of organizational change. *Journal of Management Studies, 42*(3), pp. 507-537.

This paper considers pathways of organizational change within British Rail (BR) during its long period of commercialization culminating in privatization. The Laughlin (1991) and Parker (1995a) frameworks are used to demonstrate how a new interpretative scheme supplanted the previous interpretative scheme within BR between the 1970s and privatization in the mid-1990s, leading to a fragmented organization. BR did not survive and privatization of Britain's railways remains controversial. The study demonstrates that without the earlier changes in interpretive scheme from 'social railway' to 'business railway' to 'profitable businesses, and the associated changes in design archetypes and sub-systems, privatization would have been both less tempting and less feasible. It is intended that the approach developed here to analyze organizational change in BR should be applicable to the study of other privatizations and to other forms of organizational change in both the public and private sectors.

Subject Terms:

> Organizational change
> Privatization
> Organizational structure
> Public sector
> Change management
> Corporatization
> Adaptability (Psychology)

Van de Ven, A. H., & Poole, M. S. (1995, Jul.). Explaining development and change in organizations. *The Academy of Management Review, 20*(3), pp. 510-540.

This article introduces four basic theories that may serve as building blocks to expand processes and change in organizations: life cycle, teleogy, dialectics, and evolution. These four theories represent different sequences of change events that are driven by different conceptual motors and operate at different organizational levels. This article indicates the circumstances when each theory applies and proposes how interplay among the theories of change and development in organizational life.

Subject Terms:

Industrial organization
Organizational change
Organizational growth
Organizational structure
Organizational sociology
Industrial management
Organizational death
Innovation adoption
Social change

Van de Ven, A. H., & Poole, M. S. (2005). Alternative approaches for studying organizational change. *Organization Studies*, pp. 1377-1404.

Scholars hold different views about whether organizations consist of things or processes and about variance or process methods for conducting research. By combining these two dimensions, we develop a typology of four approaches for studying organizational change. Although the four approaches may be viewed as opposing or competing views, we see them as being complementary. Each approach focuses on different questions and provides a different — but partial — understanding of organizational change. We argue that coordinating the pluralistic insights from the four approaches provides a richer understanding of organization change than any one approach provides by itself.

Subject Terms:

> Organizational change
> Organizational structure
> Research
> Management science
> Organization adaptability (Psychology)

Van de Ven, A. H., & Sun, K. (2011, Aug.). Breakdowns in implementing models of organizational change. *Academy of Management Perspectives, 25*(3), pp. 58-74.

Practice theories of implementing change are lagging behind process theories of organizational change and development. To address this gap, this paper examines common breakdowns in implementing four process models of organization change: teleology (planned change), life cycle (regulated change), dialectics (conflictive change), and evolution (competitive change). Change agents typically respond to these breakdowns by taking actions to correct people and organizational processes so they conform to their model of change. Although this strategy commands most of the attention in the literature, we argue that in many situations managers and scholars might do better if they reflected on and revised their mental model to fit the change journey that is unfolding in their organization.

Van Tonder, C. L. (2004). Below-the-surface and powerful: The emerging notion of organization identity. *Organization Development Journal*, *22*(2), pp. 68-78.

The article discusses the emerging notion of organization identity. View that emerging theory and initial empirical research indicate that the "below-the-surface" phenomenon of organization identity offers an avenue to the organization development (OD) practitioner; Perception that identity interventions in and of themselves build organizational capacity that would extend the life expectancy of organization.

Subject Terms:

    Corporate image
    Organizational behavior
    Organizational change
    Organizational structure

Varney, G. H. (2006). Challenges facing the field of organization development: An academic perspective. *Organization Development Journal, 24*(1), pp. 101-105.

Organization Development (OD) has been going through an identity crisis with many professional in the field questioning if OD will survive. A group of academics and practitioners met at a 'Summit' in April 2006 to study the challenges facing the field. They concluded that to survive their needs to be more research on the change process, build bridges between academics and practitioners, we need to talk up the field, promote OD as a profession, improve OD educational processes, and think international.

Subject Terms:

> Organizational change
> Research
> Organizational behavior
> Professional
> Organization
> Planning

Vignone, M. (2012). Family, buildings, and wars. *OD Practitioner*, *44*(1), pp. 34-37.

The article focuses on conceptual metaphor theory, analysis, and their importance in attaining organizational change and success. It notes that conceptual metaphors served as powerful and useful tools for organization development professionals. It mentions that both conceptual metaphor theory and analysis have positive impacts on various aspects in the areas of organizational change, leader's communication, and understanding organizational culture.

Subject Terms:

    Organizational change
    Success in business
    Communication in organizations
    Change agents

Virkkunen, J., & Miettinen, R. (2005). Epistemic objects, artefacts and
organizational change, *Organization, 12(3), pp. 437-456.*

One of the key concepts of the neo-institutional studies of organizations has been
routine—an established, rule-governed pattern of action. The concept of routine
creates difficulties when used for making sense of the emergence of new practices
or change in organizations and institutions. There are two reasons for this. First,
routine was introduced originally to account for the continuity of organizational
life. Second, it is based on theories of action and behavior that focus exclusively on
the pre-reflective and embodied aspects of human practice. This paper seeks an
alternative approach by using the concepts of epistemic object and artifact
mediation of human activity. It argues that representational artifacts, such as
concepts and models, are instrumental in inducing change in human practices.
Using the work of occupational health and safety inspectors as an example, it is
shown how a practice or set of routines is made into an object of enquiry in order to
generate a working hypothesis for an alternative practice. The hypothesis is further
objectified by designing a set of informational tools and procedures that carry on
the new practice.

Subject Terms:

    Organizational change
    Epistemic

Vogelsang, J. (2010). From the editor. *OD Practitioner, 42*(3), *pp.* 1.

An introduction to the journal is presented in which the editor elaborates the articles published within the issue including one on strength assessment tools, another on the essence of preferences, social values, and predispositions of individuals, and one on evaluation of staff.

Subject Terms:

    Organizational effectiveness
    Employee – Rating of

Vogelsang, J. (2012). Speaking of change. *OD Practitioner, 44*(1), *pp.* 1.

An introduction is presented in which the editor discusses various reports within the issue on topics including the changes essential in operating a global organization, the role of metaphors in these changes, and the ways on how to measure the effect of organization development (OD) processes.

Subject Terms:

Organizational change

Vukotich, G. (2010). The 360° process. *OD Practitioner, 42*(3), *pp.* 24-29.

The article elaborates the 360° Feedback, a tool for nurturing organizational effectives. The said feedback strategy is used for performance appraisal or rating of employees, job progression, and career development. It discusses the stages that executives must consider in implementing the 360° Feedback. It also offers an example of career plan of action out from the result of the feedback.

Subject Terms:

> 360-degree feedback (Rating of employees)
> Employees – Rating of
> Job performance
> Organizational effectiveness

Wallis, S. E. (2010). Appreciating the unpredictable: A case study on questions. *Organization Development Journal, 28(2), pp.* 73-88.

A case study is presented describing a consulting engagement where three unseasoned organization development consultants help a small manufacturing firm heal a rift between management and labor by facilitating the creation of a shared values statement. While some results were to be expected, others were rather surprising. The insights from this experience suggest a relationship between engagement style and the amount of "successful surprise" that emerges within the client organization. Additional insights suggest how O.D. consultants might be more effective change enablers through "scaffolding" the inquiry process - an approach normally used in education.

Subject Terms:

> Case studies
> Qualitative research
> Consultants
> Business enterprises
> Organizational behavior
> Consulting firms
> Values
> Scaffolding (Teaching method)
> Comprehensive instruction (Reading)

Walton, E. J., & Dawson, S. (2001). Managers' perceptions of criteria of organizational effectiveness. *Journal of Management Studies, 38*(2), *pp.* 173-199.

This research explores managerial perceptions of organizational effectiveness whether they have similarities with perceptions of academics, and with the competing values model of organizational effectiveness (Quinn and Rohrbaugh, 1983). The results suggest that the same values organize the patterning of effectiveness criteria in a cohesion-based solution for managers and academics. Yet, this cohesion model has inadequate explanatory power for managers' perceptions and shows no relationship with either their experience or organizational preferences. In contrast, a conflict-based solution provides adequate explanatory power for managers and relates to their experience and to organizational preferences. If managers play any part in influencing effectiveness in organizations, then incorporating their views into models of organizational effectiveness is therefore likely to improve our understanding of organizational functioning.

Subject Terms:

> Organizational effectiveness
> Industrial efficiency
> Industrial management
> Organizational sociology research
> Exclusive ability (Management)
> Performance standards
> Strategic planning
> Business planning
> Leadership
> Employee motivation
> Incentives in industry
> Management
> Organizational behavior
> Research

Warrick, D. D. (2006). Teaching and championing O.D.: Designing an introductory course for students and managers. *Organization Development Journal, 24*(3), *pp.* 92-97.

The article focuses on teaching and promoting organizational development and change (ODC) can be made next to leadership skills, skills in ODC. The author argues that there is the need for education and training on organizational development in colleges and private and public sector organizations. He argues that It is time for those involved in ODC to take a stronger leadership role in clarifying and promoting ODC and in designing and teaching high impact introductory courses.

Subject Terms:

Leadership
Organizational change
Organizational behavior
Organizational sociology
Organizational structure
Organizational commitment

Warrick, D. D., & Mueller, J. (2010). Reinventing boards. *OD Practitioner*, *42*(1), *pp.* 15-20.

The article reports on the effort of the Organization Development (OD) to reinvent boards so that they may be effective partners in building successful organizations. It notes that the board plays an important role in governing, transformation and contributes to the success of the organization. The OD practitioner urges the board to reinvent themselves and invest in training. By providing training to the boards, it would prepare them to upgrade their performance.

Subject Terms:

      Organizational change
      Organization
      Management
      Organizational structure
      Organizational growth
      Education

Watkins, K. E., & Golembiewski, R. T. (1995, Jan.). Rethinking orgazniational development for the learning organizational. *Interntional Journal of Organizational Analysis (1993-2002), 3*(1), *pp.* 86-101.

The article examines the concept of organization development (OD) for learning organizations. The author also mentions application of organization development to learning organizations; emphasis of OD; and definition of learning organization.

Subject Terms:

Organizational learning

Weick, K. E., & Quinn, R. E. (1999). Organizational change and development . *Annual Review of Psychology, 50*(1), *pp.* 361-386.

The article explains factors affecting psychological response to organizational changes and development. Concerns over the tempo of change, characteristic rate, rhythm and pattern of work; episodic change contrasted with continuous change based on implied metaphors; episodic change following sequence freeze-rebalance-refreeze.

Subject Terms:

Organizational change – Psychological aspects

Weidner II, C. (2004). A brand in dire straits: Organization development at sixty. *Organization Development Journal, 22*(2), *pp.* 37-47.

Summarizes organization development's evolution and applied OD truisms to itself, outlines the change resources and processes required to remedy the situation and points to the quality of OD practice, its brand equity and its content domain as requiring urgent attention. The author mentions implications for future theory, research and for primary stakeholders.

Subject Terms:

    Organizational change
    Organizational behavior
    Brand equity
    Stockholders
    Organization

Wenger, E. C., & Snyder, W. M. (2000). Communities of practice: The organizational frontier. *Harvard Business Review, 78*(1), *pp.* 139-145.

A new organizational form is emerging in companies that run on knowledge: the community of practice. In addition, for this expanding universe of companies, communities of practice promise to radically galvanize knowledge sharing, learning, and change. A community of practice is a group of people informally bound together by shared expertise and passion for a joint enterprise. People in companies form them for a variety of reasons--to maintain connections with peers when the company reorganizes; to respond to external changes such as the rise of e-commerce; or to meet new challenges when the company changes strategy. Regardless of the circumstances that give rise to communities of practice, their members inevitably, share knowledge in free-flowing, creative ways that foster new approaches to problems. Over the past five years, the authors have seen communities of practice improve performance at companies as diverse as an international bank, a major car manufacturer, and a U.S. government agency. Communities of practice can drive strategy, generate new lines of business, solve problems, promote the spread of best practices, develop people's skills, and help companies recruit and retain talent. The paradox of such communities is that although they are self-organizing and thus resistant to supervision and interference, they do require specific managerial efforts to develop them and integrate them into an organization. Only then can they be fully leveraged. The authors explain the steps managers need to take in order to get communities going-and to sustain them so they can become a central part of their companies' success. INSET: Communities in Action.

Subject Terms:

> Teams in the workplace
> Group decision making
> Group problem solving
> Business networks
> Organizational behavior
> Industrial management
> Industrial organization
> Business planning
> Best practices
> Organizational structure

Whatley, L. R. (2011). A new model for family owned business succession. *Organization Development Journal*, *29*(4), *pp.* 21-32.

The Organizational Development (OD) literature has predominantly focused on larger institutions. However, Family Owned Businesses (FOBs) also contribute significantly to the economy and to society. Historically, the success rates of FOB succession are low and questions arise as to the role and importance, if any, of the OD practitioner and scholar in aiding succession planning and transfer within FOBs. This paper explores the existing academic literature on FOB succession, and using the insight gained from assisting FOBs in successful succession, the author merges two existing models on FOB succession to create a new model, thus enhancing our approach to OD interventions in this dynamic field. The new model combines the Integrative Model of Effective FOB Succession (Le Breton-Miller, Miller, & Steier, 2008) and the FOB Knowledge Accumulation Model (Chirico, 2008) in an attempt to adopt the strengths and address the weaknesses of each approach. The effectiveness of this new model is demonstrated by a case study.

Subject Terms:

    Family-owned business enterprises
    Organizational change
    Organizational structure
    Success in business
    Business planning
    Business development

Wheatley, M. J. (2003). *Organizational Development at Work: Conversations on the values, applications, and future of OD.* San Fracisco: Pfeiffer.

The book in this series is intended to be cutting-edge, state-of-art, innovative approaches to organization change and development. They are written for and by practitioners interested in new approaches to facilitating effective organization change. They are geared to providing both theory and advice on practical applications.

Subject Terms:

Organizational change

Whiting, S. W., Maynes, T. D., Podsakoff, N. P., & Podsakoff, P. M. (2012).
Effects of message, source, and context on evaluations of employee voice
behavior. *Journal of Applied Psychology, 97*(1), *pp.* 159-182.

Although employee voice behavior is expected to have important organizational
benefits, research indicates that employees voicing their recommendations for
organizational change may be evaluated either positively or negatively by
observers. A review of the literature suggests that the perceived efficacy of voice
behaviors may be a function of characteristics associated with the (a) source, (b)
message, and (c) context of the voice event. In this study, we manipulated variables
from each of these categories based on a model designed to predict when voice will
positively or negatively influence raters' evaluations of an employee's performance.
To test our model, we conducted three laboratory studies in which we manipulated
two source factors (voice expertise and trustworthiness), two message factors
(recommending a solution and positively vs. negatively framing the message), and
two context factors (timing of the voice event and organizational norms for
speaking up vs. keeping quiet). We also examined the mediating effects of liking,
prosaically motives, and perceptions that the voice behavior was constructive on
the relationships between the source, message, and context factors and performance
evaluations. Generally speaking, we found that at least one of the variables from
each category had an effect on performance evaluations for the voice and that most
of these effects were indirect, operating through one or more of the mediators.
Implications for theory and future research are discussed.

Subject Terms:

    Research
    Organizational change
    Employees
    Industrial psychology
    Voice
    Performance

Wickhorst, V., & Geroy, G. (2006). Physical communication and organization development. *Organization Development Journal, 24*(3), *pp.* 54-63.

The field of Organization Development (O.D.) is broad and incorporates a number of disciplines. Due to the complexity of factors, the field of O.D. tends to specialize in the interpersonal aspects within organizations. The position presented and supported in this article is that manipulation of the physical environment is an effective tool for the O.D. professional. The article presents research in architectural and space design, as well as in proxemics and physical symbols in the environment. Manipulation of these variables has proven to produce positive affect and outcomes in organizational settings.

Subject Terms:

Organizational behavior
Organizational change
Organizational commitment
Organizational learning
Organizational socialization
Organizational sociology

Wirtenberg, J., Lipsky, D., Abrams, L., Conway, M., & Slepian, J. (2007). The future of organization development: Enabling sustainable business performance through people. *Organization Development Journal, 25*(2), *pp.* P11-22.

The following synthesis of a global business leader survey conducted by the research team of the Global Committee on the Future of Organization Development is juxtaposed with a case study from Sony Electronics to illustrate how effective organization development practices can be applied to, add value to, and enhance a world-class company. Survey results reveal that leaders across a wide range of industries see increasing opportunities for OD-related work that is critical to the future of business and society. In some areas, that organizational leaders consider critically important, there are some considerable rooms to improve the effectiveness of the organization. The sustainability of their businesses, and the field of OD offers some of its greatest strengths in these very areas, this paper is a call for action for Organizational Development practitioners to help close the gaps that are identified in this study.

Subject Terms:

  Organizational change
  Research
  Business development
  Business
  Organizational behavior
  International business enterprises
  Globalization
  Survey

Woodman, R. (2006). Building ODC as an academic discipline: Research in ODC. *Organization Development Journal, 24*(3), *pp.* 98-99.

The article discusses the challenge faced by the organizational development and change in terms of contributing important research in the organizational sciences is a difficult one. He points out that there is a prescriptive set of actions to offer in organizational leadership. He suggests actions in three areas that might be useful for organizational change.

Subject Terms:

> Leadership
> Organizational change
> Organizational behavior
> Organizational sociology
> Organizational structure
> Organizational commitment

Worley, C. (2006). Building O.D.C. as an academic discipline: Authorship in ODC. *Organization Development Journal, 24*(3), *pp.* 90-91.

The article discusses the challenges facing the organizational development and change as an academic discipline. The author points out that from an authorship perspective, the lack of boundaries means that any number of reputable and not-so-reputable outlets of publication exists. He argues that organizational developments and change is not respected as a discipline.

Subject Terms:

>   Organizational change
>   Organizational behavior
>   Organizational sociology
>   Organizational structure
>   Organizational commitment

Yaeger, T. F., & Sorensen, P. F. (2004). Meet Vladimiras Obrastovas, Chairman of the 24th OD World Congress. *Organization Development Journal, 22*(2), *pp.* 104-107.

Presents an interview with Vladimiras Obrazcovas, Chairman of the 24th Organization Development (OD) World Congress. Description of his position at the Lithuanian University of Law; Initial involvement in OD; Description of his most unique OD project; Preview of and plans for the 12th OD World Congress.

Subject Terms:

> Organizational change
> Conferences & conventions
> Law teachers
> Congresses

Yaeger, T. F., & Sorensen, P. F. (2006). Strategic organization development: Past to present. *Organization Development Journal, 24*(4), *pp.* 10-16.

Twenty years ago, there was considerable concern that O.D. needed to become more strategic. This article reviews the evolution of O.D. from the concerns voiced decades ago to today's reality. In this article, we review definitions of what it means to be strategic and we review key changes in the field that reflect the key characteristics of strategic O.D. These key areas include references in the literature to strategic O.D., international and global O.D., the role of HRM, organization design, information technology, ethics and positive change.

Subject Terms:

    Organizational change
    Organization
    Management
    Personnel management
    Information technology
    Professional ethics
    Strategic planning

Yaeger, T. F., & Sorensen, P. F. (2009). Today's challenging times and the role of OD. *OD Practitioner*, *41*(2), *pp.* 50-54.

The article presents a case, which challenges the role of an organization development (OD) practitioner. It highlights the situation of Insuranco who is dealing with the impact of the economic crisis, and as well as the challenge of the company's OD director. It outlines the advises and recommendations of the three highly experienced OD practitioners which include Rob Kjar of a Japanese Pharmaceutical company, Dawn Newman of Boeing Company, and Neesa Sweet of Braided River Group, in addressing the company's situation. It points out that the current situation of Insuranco serve as a challenge for OD professionals to demonstrate their real contribution to the organization.

Subject Terms:

Organizational change
Organizational behavior
Management
Organizational structure
Leadership

Yaeger, T. F., & Sorensen, P. F. (2010). Prescribing a healthy dose of OD for healthcare. *OD Practitioner*, *42*(3), *pp.* 53-56.

The article presents questions and answers on furthering organization development in a healthcare system.

Subject Terms:

       Organizational change
       Organizational effectiveness
       Health services administration
       Medical care
       Strategic planning

Yaeger, T. F., & Sorensen, P. F. (2011). OD in Africa. *OD Practitioner*, *43*(3), *pp.* 50-54.

The article presents a case study on organization development (OD) applications in Africa. The study considers three African OD experts addressing OD including Chiku Malunga's understanding of African proverbs to be applied by OD practitioner in organizations and to boost performance and the use of OD programs in Ghana like consensus building by Betty Nanor Arthur. It also discusses Dalitso Samson Sulamoyo's factors that must be considered by OD professionals to bring change in an organization.

Subject Terms:

    Case studies
    Organizational change
    Job performance
    Consensus (Social sciences)

Yaeger, T. F., & Sorensen, P. F. (2011, Winter). Organizational development's role when going global. *OD Practioner, 43*(1), *pp.* 48-52.

The article offers the insights of various global experts regarding the organizational development (OD) of Pharma Inc. Executive vice president Nazneen Razi of Jones Lang LaSalle Inc. discusses the role of OD and human resource (HR) in the pharmaceutical industry in India. President Dalitso S. Sulamoyo of Illinois Association of Community Action Agencies states that OD approach on the proposed expansion and growth of Pharma Inc. in Africa involves identification of local African practitioners.

Subject Terms:

Organizational change
Organizational behavior

Yaeger, T. F., & Sorensen, P. F. (2012). Exploring large group interventions. *OD Practitioner, 44*(1), *pp.* 52-55.

A case study is presented on Kerry, an organization development (OD) professional who needs support and is seeking for an OD mentor. It notes that Kerry has raised several questions including the top ten tools and techniques required for OD operations, the approaches essential in promoting organizational change, and the data needed in measuring the outcome of OD initiative. It mentions that engagement approaches are necessary for the commitment and alignment of diverse stakeholders.

Subject Terms:

Case studies
Organizational change
Mentoring in business
Stakeholders
Change agents

Yeganeh, B., & Kolb, D. (2009). Mindfulness and experiential learning. *OD Practitioner, 41*(3), *pp.* 13-18.

The article explores the on the role of being mindfulness as a tool to assists learners in unlocking their full learning potential in organization. It discusses how mindfulness techniques can enhance the learning and tools for practice in an organization and mentions that learning style describes the unique ways through the learning cycle based on their learning need. It then asserts that mindfulness is a tool to enhance life by reducing automaticity and is experiential learning that can be cultivated in an organization without mandating employees to commit meditation practices.

Subject Terms:

Organization
Management
Communication in organizations
Organizational sociology
Organizational learning
Organizational behavior
Active learning
Experimental learning
Learning
Communities of practice

Yeo, R. K. (2009). Electronic government as a strategic intervention in organizational change processes. *Journal of Change Management, 9*(3), *pp.* 271-304.

The article explores electronic government as a change intervention initiative in the Sabah State public administration. It discusses its influence on organizational strategy, structure and performance, and argues that people are the active carriers of institutional meanings and actions that facilitate change. The study was conducted based on a qualitative research design involving in depth interviewing with 18 participants and data triangulation from other secondary sources. Findings suggest that electronic government was a transformative approach to organizational change and development. Taking the Sabah civil service to a globalized level, it added broader dimension to the organization's strategic direction with a focus on long-term goals. The transformation began with the creation of new social structures where power relations were distributed across employee levels. This had an impact on the notion of leadership as the introduction of electronic government had led to a decentralization of decision-making and action taking. Electronic government created opportunities for work collaboration and knowledge co-construction through various communities of practices. It opened up new avenues for information to be used, disseminated and retained, improving work innovation and job satisfaction. The study offers implications for theory where the complex and dynamic interrelations between organizational strategy, structure and people are explored. The focus is not on technology; it hinges on the potential for cross-boundary collaboration and participation in the context of a developing country such as the Sabah State where there are rural areas to which the public administration needs to reach out. In such circumstances, electronic government can become as much a vision as a tool.

Subject Terms:

> Public administration
> Organizational change
> Civil service
> Internet in public administration
> Organizational aims & objectives

Zimmerman, J. (2004). Leading organizational change is like climbing a mountain. *The Educational Forum, 68*(3), *pp.* 234-242.

Leading organizational change is like climbing a mountain. Transformational leaders must prepare to lead change, understand the process and nature of change, and provide the essential gear so that those involved can be successful. The author draws on the literature and personal experiences as a hiker and change leader to provide a guide for leading organizational change.

Subject Terms:

Organizational change
Educational leadership

Žydžiūnaitė, V., & Lepaitė, D. (2010). Aspects of social processes within a business organization for a positive development of organizational behavior. *Issues of Business & Law, pp.* 274-84.

This article presents research on the initiation of changes in organizational behavior, integration of research consultants and identification of managers' and employees' perceptions about the parameters of a collegial model in order to plan social actions by replacing an autocratic model within an organization with a collegial one. The research problem is a survey concerning the change of organizational behavior when a business company seeks to maintain the quality of services and an effective ratio between the development of business and the quantity of human resources. The focus of the research is a positive development of a case study of a single organization. The aim of the research is to explore the development direction of a case study of a single organization by highlighting aspects for a positive organizational development. The research objectives are: (1) to evaluate the perspectives of human resource development within an organization (the potential of employees such as employees' self-orientation; orientation to colleagues; working environment; organizational administration) as a premise for organizational development towards a collegial model by striving to involve and stipulate the participation of employees in the achievement of organizational results; and (2) to evaluate the needs of the employees for self-realization by matching it with organizational aims. The strength of organizational behavior is the organization of working activity, which refers to procedural aspects of work. The weakness of organizational behavior is the internal commitment and responsibility of the employees. Discrepancy of organizational behavior is attributed to the employees' tendency to evaluate the same aspect of organizational behavior equally positively and negatively.

Subject Terms:
  Case studies
  Organizational behavior
  Customer services
  Organizational change
  Corporate culture

374

Topic index